WHATEVER HAPPENED TO THAT LITTLE FOREIGN GIRL?

Whatever Happened to that Little Foreign Girl?

Angelika Bailey

Copyright © 2024 by Angelika Bailey
All rights reserved. No part of this book may be reproduced in any manner whatsoever without written permission except in the case of brief quotations embodied in critical articles and reviews.
First Printing, 2025

 A catalogue record for this book is available from the National Library of Australia

Published by: Newgrange Damaras
Editing: Eddie Albrecht, Pickawoowoo Publishing Group
Typesetting & Layout: Pickawoowoo Publishing Group

Paperback ISBN: 9781763829701
E-Book ISBN: 9781763829718

Print & Channel Distribution: Lightning Source / IngramSpark

For Mick Bailey. The love of my life.

Acknowledgements

I sincerely thank my sister Barbara, for her encouragement in bringing this story to life.
Without her powers of persuasion and the belief that it had merit, I may never have had the courage to begin, let alone complete this work.

***

This is a work of creative non-fiction. It is my life story. All of the events are true to the best of my memory. Some names and identifying features have been changed to protect the identity of certain parties.
I have used online resources to check facts in the telling of my story. Events that occurred during the decades covered in the telling are clearly recorded in the public domain.
I in no way represent any company, corporation or brand mentioned here.

Contents

Dedication   v
Acknowledgements   vii

1 Berlin, Charlottenburg - Germany   1
2 Western Australia   8
3 Darwin - Northern Territory   38
4 A Change of Direction   76
5 Western Australia - A Fresh Start   113
6 Gelorup - The Struggle Years   131
7 Then the Parents Left Home   142
8 The Western Darling Downs   174
9 Back in Western Australia   200

About the Author   209

1

Berlin, Charlottenburg - Germany

Following the heavy Allied bombing during the years of WWII and the shelling by Soviet forces during the Battle of Berlin, combined with the damage inflicted by the *Wehrmacht* prior to surrendering at the end of the war in 1945, the vibrant and cosmopolitan city of Berlin, once the capital of Prussia, then the capital of a unified Germany, known for its cultural scenes, intellectualism and architectural splendour, lay in ruins. As the *Wehrmacht* retreated, they had blown up bridges, weirs, power stations and other infrastructure, flooding the city subway system where thousands of citizens were sheltering and consequently drowned. Once grand buildings now stood like hollow shells with piles of rubble at their feet. The demolition to make sites safe and cleanup was underway but rebuilding had not yet begun, Berlin's future was still in *limbo*.

It was here in war-torn Berlin - Charlottenburg, on the 4th of May 1947 (which was a very cold Sunday evening with late snow still on the ground) that I entered this world, the first child of Paul Eugen Hoffmann and Ursula Agnes Hoffmann nee Hinz. They named me Angelika (meaning of the angels, *angelic*). My mother was a survivor of the Battle of Berlin and my father had recently returned from naval service, they were living with my grandmother who was fortunate to have an undamaged three-bedroom apartment, along with my uncle, aunt and their baby daughter.

At the end of WWII Germany was divided into four sectors, three were administered by the Western Allied Forces and one by the Soviet Occupation Forces. Berlin, the capital, was similarly divided. Relations broke down during the ensuing years and the "Iron Curtain" fell across other European nations as the USSR's grip on power strengthened. Tensions further rose when the West didn't bow to Soviet demands, resulting in the 'Cold War'; the Soviet Union ordering a total blockade of Berlin. Berlin thus became an island within the Soviet sector. The Allies began the "Berlin Airlift", a very long campaign to bring food and fuel into West Berlin. The blockade was ultimately broken in 1949, leading to the formation of West Germany, (the new capital of West Germany was named Bonn) effectively dividing the nation for many years into East and West. The Berlin Wall was put in place in 1961 and stood for 28 years.

Conditions in Berlin were harsh when I was born, father was fortunate to be working for the Allies in 1947 as a translator and driver. However, all was not well; food was still in short supply and rationed, hardship was everywhere and worsening, father's hobby of building radio sets helped, these were sold through the underground 'black market' which had been established. Then father was made redundant! Officially, because of the Allies' need to economise due to pressures to rebuild their homelands. Unofficially, (so the story goes) he was 'let go' after he was seen taking home bones meant to feed the guard dogs. Grandmother *'Oma'* would use these bones to make soup, augmented with root vegetables foraged from the fields of derelict market gardens and meager rations to feed her family.

My father's aunt Anna-Charlotte Hoffmann (*tante Annie*) was living in West Germany. She found accommodation for my father in a hostel for displaced persons and employment, so he left for West Germany in August 1948, crossing at Marienburg-Helmstedt (checkpoint Alpha) the shortest route from Berlin through what was now East

Germany to the West. My father then having secured both employment and accommodation for our family, enabled my mother to pack up and we joined him in November 1948. I was now 18 months old.

The checkpoint was established in 1945 – the demarcation line between the Soviet and British occupation zones. Road and rail access between West Berlin and West Germany was informally allowed, the crossing remained possible during the Cold War for those living in the western sector, travellers were required to carry their identity card, passport and visa. The arrangement was mostly respected albeit with periodic interruptions and harassment of travellers. The worst disruption was in 1948 during the Berlin Blockade.

The story of our crossing at the checkpoint was often retold, my mother and uncle re-living the event at family gatherings. My uncle accompanied us to the end of the railway line at the border dividing East and West Germany. At this point the locomotive and driver were changed over for the next stage of the journey, passengers were required to alight and go through the checkpoint while this change occurred. Mother now alone with her suitcase and me in a baby-carriage, full of trepidation and fear born from her experiences at the hands of Soviet Forces during the fall of Berlin, entered the checkpoint manned by armed guards from the Soviet Occupation Force. The checkpoint consisted of little more than a temporary wooden building, manned by the border patrol, her 'papers' were inspected and stamped, her meager belongings searched, the next item for scrutiny was the baby-carriage, a guard shone his torch into the pram, this woke me and I began to cry, without further searching or delay he waved us through, we could continue our journey. Did divine providence have a hand in this, is there a path mapped out for us to follow?

Our now reunited family settled in the Ruhr-Rhine region of Westphalia, West Germany in a town named Witten-Annen. My father had found work in a steel mill, initially we shared an attic room in a 'Mansion' which had a garden. My memories from this time are still 'learnt'. I was told that I swapped my doll for a licorice lollypop which upset my mother greatly. As part of the reconstruction, all the men were required to work a certain number of hours on housing projects, we were eventually allocated a two-room upper-floor apartment, comprising of an eat-in kitchen and a living room. My parents slept on a sofa bed in the living room and my bed folded against the wall during the day. A bathroom and hall closet completed the apartment. There was also a communal attic and a basement.

There were happy times with my parents, I remember my grandmother '*Oma*' coming to visit, outings to various towns and the village life, markets and a special visit to mother's relatives on a farm, a visit to great aunt Annie, there were other children to play with in an expanding world. I also remember being shut into the hall closet for some misdemeanor or other, focusing on a crack of light where the door met the lock, or being shut into the bathroom, smearing the walls with soft soap to pass the time, receiving a spanking for my efforts. Also father tossing my toy dog into the stove firebox because I hadn't picked up the toys, opening the firebox next morning and being heartbroken at seeing the ashes of the toy, so perfect, I reached in to retrieve it only to have it disintegrate.

I recall the changing seasons, the colours of the autumn leaves, mother making me crowns of oak leaves or daisies, Christmas wonderland, the smell of chestnuts roasting and catching snowflakes. Running home crying because all the pigeons in a neighbour's coop were suddenly headless, too young to know that birds tuck their heads under their wing when sleeping. Of being given a paper bag containing cherries, told to sit on the doorstep to eat them while my mother was getting ready for us to go shopping. The outcome not quite as intended. The cherry juice stained my skirt, so what does a 4-year-old do? I took it off, rolled it up and stuffed it into the bag along with the cherry pits. Perhaps mother saw some humour in this, she cleaned me up and we headed into town, as a special treat we went to a café, she had ice-cream but bought me a cone of whipped cream, she thought I was too young to have ice-cream.

Next are memories of starting school, a satchel and a slate tablet to write on. It was customary in Germany to give a child a cornucopia filled with sweets and treats on the first day of school, mine was almost as big as myself, fond memories of my favourite playmate, a black shaggy dog belonging to a neighbour, lying beside him in his kennel sharing sandwiches. Of picking wild blue-berries in the woods, of special birthday cakes and Easter egg hunts. Street parades with bands playing, learning to roller skate, making snowmen and tobogganing down the hillside, sitting in-front of father, who was controlling the sled, then trudging back up the hill for another run.

Early in 1953; a big announcement was made, a baby was coming to join the family, would it be a girl or a boy? I was emphatic it had to be a little sister; I would name her Barbara. I sprinkled sugar on the windowsill, to bribe the stork who would bring her, surely my wish would be granted;

My father had a bad accident at work; he'd inadvertently stepped into a pit of burning sawdust, both his feet were badly burnt. My parents unable to see a bright future with the way things were in post war Germany, began to discuss immigrating to the new world for a fresh start. America, Canada or Australia? Father saw an advertisement for assisted migration promoted by the Australian Government, he applied and we were accepted. A flurry of preparations and goodbyes followed, then we were on our way to Bremen, the departure point for Melbourne, Australia on the ship 'Castel Verde'. The start of a new phase in the life of our little family. The voyage would take four weeks and there was much anticipation of wonderful sights along the way. The ship's crew were mostly Italian.

The voyage was indeed memorable and exciting, mother and I shared a cabin with another woman and her child, father and the other menfolk slept below decks in shared accommodation. There were organized activities for the children and mischief to get into. My teddy is still swimming somewhere out in the Indian Ocean thanks to a nasty boy. He took it from me and said he would give it back if

I climbed up the ships funnel and touched the black line at the top, desperate to have my bear back I started to climb, I was 'rescued' by a ship's officer when I drew level with an upper deck, perhaps some 10 or 12 meters up, for me the sound of panicked voices of the people looking on was more terrifying than looking down. He reached out and grabbed hold of me speaking to me in Italian which I didn't understand so I panicked. Once on a firm footing, I bolted to find mother, slipped on a metal staircase, fell and lacerated my back, bleeding and crying, mother took me to the sick bay. The iodine that was painted onto the wounds stung like fire. The injustice of this whole event stung twice as badly as my bear was gone, the boy had thrown him overboard to hide his involvement, denying everything. Finally, I received a dressing down from my father, a memorable day for all the wrong reasons.

Mother was sick for most of the voyage, a combination of seasickness and pregnancy. My father kept busy teaching English language to the immigrants. I managed to stay out of harm's way for the rest of the voyage. Port Said, the Suez Canal, so narrow it felt like you could almost touch the banks, next the Red Sea Passage to Port Aden, buildings with white walls, arches and flat roofs, palm trees. Vendors, people with dark skin and exotic looking clothes in small boats coming alongside, rope ladders and baskets being dropped over the side of the ship and exotic fruits being brought onboard. The first sight of watermelon; tasting the first slice, so sweet and juicy! Then on to Colombo, where the ship docked for supplies.

Next came the Indian Ocean, such a vast expanse of sea and sky, heat, real heat and sunshine, swimming in the ship's pool, flying fish and dolphins swimming alongside the ship, celebrations crossing the Equator. Australia was getting closer. As the ship neared the coast of Western Australia an announcement was made. The Western Australian government had asked for workers for the construction of the Kwinana Refinery. A ballot of passenger ID numbers was held and our number was among those drawn out, we were to disembark at Fremantle. Mother was very pleased; she really hadn't enjoyed the voyage. The ship entered 'Gage Roads' on the 7th July 1953 and we stepped onto Australian soil for the first time that afternoon.

2

Western Australia

The immigration process took some time and the new arrivals experienced Australia's biosecurity, all the lovely produce people had taken from the ship was confiscated, they were distraught, after the hardship and deprivation following the war, such waste was too much to comprehend and with the language barrier at the time it was a very confusing event. Then we were given a food parcel at the end of the line as we boarded the train for Northam's 'Holden Camp', our temporary home for the next stage of the adventure. I was eating a red apple that evening and lost my first tooth.

The camp was an interesting place, although strange. Nissin huts in rows, partitioned with half walls, open at the top and at floor level. Camp beds with wire bases that creaked, kapok pillows and mattresses, 2 grey ex-army issue blankets per person, meals in a mess hall, strange food. It smelled and tasted so different to what we were used to. Communal ablution facilities, it was July, cold and wet, it was muddy, we didn't have winter clothes, where was this land of sunshine that we had come to? Mother and I spent hours together exploring, we had a whole new world to discover. The Avon River at Northam, we fed the black and white swans and ducks, parklands with strange plants and wildflowers growing alongside the railway tracks. Playgrounds with swings, a slippery slide and climbing frame. Father was working for the State Government translating migrant's documents and trade certificates so that the families could get employment and move on to the next stage of life in Western Australia.

When this task was complete, he found employment at a timber mill in Toodyay, not very far away. Mother and I had to stay at the Camp while he got settled and found accommodation for us. Then I came down with measles so we were moved into a nicer place, a private suite in a long building with a verandah. Mother scrubbed and cleaned our room, washed curtains and polished the window panes, the opaque glass was now shining and clear, suddenly the room was much brighter. Father purchased a single burner spirit stove for us, Mother prepared familiar meals, often just by adding butter and milk to the mash and flavouring the meat dishes we collected from the dining hall. Father came to visit on weekends, he was living in a tent in Toodyay, finding his feet and trying to get settled. Eventually he rented a half house by the river in Toodyay, by now it was September 1953.

* * *

Toodyay

Our first home in Toodyay wasn't conventional, we had 3 rooms and a long verandah down one side of what had once been a single dwelling, comprising a kitchen-living room and 2 bedrooms. There was a bathroom-laundry underneath, and an outside dunny some way down a path in the back yard, not a flushing toilet, what a shock that was! The back fence ran parallel to the river bank. We spent a lot of time out on the verandah.

I was enrolled at school; my education began and so did the culture shock. Language became an issue; I picked up all the taboo words very quickly, apparently, I could swear like a trooper, although I had no idea what I was saying. For the life of me I couldn't understand why father thought I had to have my mouth washed out with soap! Must have been fun to teach the little German girl naughty words. I stood out from the other girls as my clothes and hairstyle were so different, so European. I felt like an outsider and was a curiosity to the local children. I was the little foreign girl, alone most of the time, I went on long walks exploring down by the river, along road-sides and into paddocks. The road verge to the cemetery was a wonderland of flowers that spring, naturalised bulbs sprang up in abundance, there were hedges of dog-roses, the bush was full of amazing wildflowers, lambs were born and played in the paddocks, it was lovely.

Some of the townsfolk were welcoming and tried to find out about these newcomers to their community, but in the 1950's immigrants were aliens and memories of WWII were still very fresh in the minds of many, so there was a high degree of suspicion among the population. The family who lived down the street were friendly, had a daughter my age who invited me to their house, they had a refrigerator and gave us green ice blocks as an afterschool treat.

It was a long walk to school each morning but there was fruit on trees which overhung front fences, some of which I'd never seen, like figs, loquats and pomegranates, which fascinated me. Then I came down with whooping cough. Another strange experience; the doctor prescribed medication that came in a capsule. Mother didn't understand that it was to be taken whole, so broke each capsule open and administered the dose, it was so foul tasting it usually came back up rather quickly, then she tried mixing it with honey.

Our packing crates from Germany arrived and were unpacked, the strangest item that came out was a toboggan, perhaps it would have been useful had we gone on to Melbourne, but it was a strange thing to have in Western Australia in summer, it was later converted to a billy-cart. Father started to build our furniture from timber that he got from the mill where he worked. It was all very solid and heavy, being mostly made of jarrah and Masonite. The packing crates were converted into lower kitchen cupboards, the lid became a shelf and mother hung checkered curtains on the front.

I still have one of the cupboards he made to this day in my garden shed. The best thing he built was a cot for the baby whose arrival time was getting closer. Mother made curtains, quilts and cushions to dress our home. It was getting hotter; we were about to experience our first Australian summer. She sewed baby clothes, clothes for my dolls, made me pretty dresses, she purchased meters of muslin and flannelette, sewed nappies for the baby, made calico sheets and pillow cases. Her sewing machine ran overtime, in the evenings, she would embroider the clothes and linen she'd made for me and the baby.

On the 24th of November 1953, an ambulance stopped at school, I was summoned to find mother sitting in the back. She told me that arrangements had been made for me to spend the night at school, Saint Aloysius Convent of Mercy was a boarding school and that father would come and collect me the next day. Later that afternoon my baby sister was born at Northam Hospital. As excited as I was, longing to see and hold her, I was to be disappointed, children were only allowed to look at their new siblings through a window from the verandah of the hospital.

She was named Barbara; after all I had insisted that was to be her name and Elizabeth after our maternal grandmother. Barbara was a miracle, I couldn't wait for her to grow up, she was so pretty with golden red curls, shiny like a new penny, she drew comments and praise wherever we went. My very own sister, dreams can come true. Having no other family in Australia, our parents asked a new friend to be Barbara's godfather, after the ceremony, we went to his house for afternoon tea, his wife had made fresh Danish pastries, what a wonderful treat that was. This couple were considerably older than our parents, they had an adult daughter, we were invited to the girl's wedding, she looked so lovely as a bride.

Sometime later we went to a funeral, I remember playing with other children picking flowers and running about among the headstones. Being so young I didn't understand much of what was happening. Some years later I asked mother about it and learnt that the young bride had died from leukemia, not very long after her marriage. A fresh start in a new land doesn't mean that tragedy won't find you, how awful that must have been for those people.

There was more to come, 1953 wasn't done yet. We moved house on Christmas Eve to the other side of town, this time to a cottage, part of the mill complex where father worked, rent lower, in exchange for caretaker duties. The cottage was weatherboard with an iron roof, had front and back verandahs, 4 main rooms, living-dining, master bedroom, at the back was the kitchen separated from the bathroom and laundry by a small hallway. The back verandah had an earth floor. The front verandah was partly enclosed to form a sleepout which was for the children. A garage, with a lean-to woodshed, an outhouse dunny, a separate smaller single room hut with a verandah to the side completed the complex. This had once been the mill Manager's residence and office.

This cottage was much closer to school, along the way was a community of migrant families who had arrived in Australia earlier to work on the railways. It was fun getting to know this diverse group, there was common ground, they had mainly come from other parts of eastern Europe, were displaced persons due to the war. One event still evokes a pleasant memory, it was the christening of twin baby boys. After the feasting, the festivities really got underway, there was Cossack dancing on the table and folk dancing by the women, wearing traditional dresses. It was a wonderful party.

Our parents fenced an area by the side of the cottage and planted a garden with a lawn for us to play on. Our paths were covered in a thick layer of sawdust so that they wouldn't be muddy after rain. Father put railings with flower boxes around the front verandah and mother planted geraniums in them. Father hung a swing for us on one of the giant gum trees in front of our cottage and built us a seesaw. We had chickens and fresh eggs, regularly visited local farms to get fresh fruit and honey. I fell in love with the idea of living on a farm, I watched how the cows were milked, how cream was separated from the milk and churned into butter, I collected eggs and helped feed chickens. Helped take scraps to the pigpens and fed the pigs. Played with the piglets, puppies and hayshed kittens. I loved the annual agricultural show, the outdoor picture show and country dances in the town hall where children always came along.

Small town life in the 1950s was still really unsophisticated and 240volt electricity wasn't available everywhere. Our cottage was lit by 32volt power inside but we used kerosene lanterns outside, cooking was done on a wood fired stove and refrigeration consisted of a water bag and a Coolgardie cooler on the back verandah. Later an ice chest, finally a kerosene fridge. In the heat of summer mother cooked on a pair of spirit stoves. She tried her hand at making grape jelly, it was so hot that the jelly didn't set, it was semi-set early in the mornings, the Coolgardie cooler just wasn't cold enough. Still; the jelly tasted lovely on pancakes.

Our laundry was done in a copper and on a washboard in cement wash tubs, a wringer mangle between the tubs being the only helper. No Hills Hoist, just a prop line over red earth which could and did blow down during 'willy willy's or 'dust devils' - heat generated wind funnels that skip along bare earth collecting surface debris forming a column of dust, a strong woman was brought to tears more than once. Ironing was done with flat irons heated on the wood stove and hot water was delivered via a chip heater alongside the bathtub. It was my job to ensure there were sufficient chips and twigs to fuel the heater for hot water for our bath. Father often had to spend time soldering holes in the tub to stop it leaking.

To improve their financial position mother worked picking grapes in the summer of 1954-55. A family friend who had a baby girl a few months older than my sister was taking care of Barbara while mother was working in the vineyard. There was an outbreak of gastro-enteritis that summer, both of the babies got sick, I can still remember having to give boiled water with glucose to Barbara to keep her hydrated. When she started to recover, she was allowed to have strained orange juice, our friend's little girl died, it was so sad. Another family shattered, after becoming displaced during WWII, and moving across the world for a fresh start only to face tragedy and loss all over again.

In winter father went out paddock clearing and stump burning on local farms. He continued to renovate and improve the cottage; he built a breezeway to connect the cottage to the smaller building which had once served as the mill reception office. This link enabled it to become a bedroom and playroom for my sister and me, the sleepout became mothers sewing room. She was doing a lot of sewing, alterations and mending, word of her skill with needle and thread having spread quite far afield through her making a wonderful complete set of vestments for the catholic church. The nuns at the school I attended had commissioned them. Funds for the fabric given by members of the congregation.

Mother worked in the laundry at the convent for a time and did mending for the nuns and boarders. She sewed beautiful costumes for the end of school-year concerts. Never one to sit idle mother also did domestic work at some of the closer farms and cooked for them at shearing time. This suited her as she could take Barbara with her while I was at school. She learnt to make scones and sponge cakes, roast lamb with baked potatoes and pumpkin. Not food that had been part of our menu in Germany.

Life settled and became routine, but change was in the wind. We had all learnt the language of our new homeland and were becoming part of the fabric of our community. Most people still had difficulty pronouncing my name correctly which upset me greatly, so father thought it was a good idea to 'anglaise' it and just like that I became 'Angela'. Our parents sponsored our uncle and his family to come to Australia, they also settled in Toodyay arriving the following year. At first, they lived across the river near where we had originally lived, then moved into one of the cottages where the railway workers were housed, so were within walking distance from our home. Our cousins attended the State school.

The milkman called every other day with milk in large cans, cream in smaller ones and always gave us an extra scoop "for the cat", into our billy-can. Un-processed milk! A thick layer of cream settled on top overnight, it was often skimmed off and served with mother's apple cake for afternoon tea. The rabbit man still came with his cry 2s 6d a pair and mother always got a pair for the pot. Twice a week the dunny cart came and collected the nightsoil. We had to light a piece of paper and run it under the toilet seat in case of spiders.

The mill had shut down operations and father and uncle were now both working at the tannin factory. We continued to live by the sawmill as caretakers. We now had a car and went for drives in the country, went on holidays to the beach and picnics further afield along the river and into the foothills around Perth. Our handmade furniture was gradually replaced by factory made bedroom suites, a lounge suite, Laminex table and vinyl chairs – just like the ones you now see in old TV shows like 'Happy Days'. The furniture father had built was repurposed as outdoor furniture, we had adapted to outdoor living and camping trips.

I had been given a puppy, a little fat red kelpie, I didn't have him long, there were no vaccines against distemper. Then father got me another puppy, an Australian Terrier, this one became my best mate, he would go everywhere with me as my sister was still too young to accompany me. We weren't allowed to have dogs in the house and our cats mostly lived outside as well. One afternoon I decided to go to the local playground which was on the other side of the main street. In most country towns the main street is the thoroughfare for transports and Toodyay was no exception, I hadn't realised that my dog had followed me, I crossed the street safely but the logging truck that was coming into town hit my little dog, my dog was run over. I remember becoming hysterical, I screamed, someone came and put him out of pain. I continued to scream, a stranger tried to comfort me, I stopped screaming and started to cry, realising my little mate was gone.

I withdrew sad and lonely; spent a lot of time under the big peppercorn tree behind our cottage reading, or up at the top of the hill by the town reservoir's spillway among the everlasting daisies, or just walking in bushland or along the riverbank, no particular destination in mind. Barbara still just a toddler, happily playing with her dolls and kittens, our flock of chickens following her about. Eventually time healed my grief, or was it the news that my dog was the sire of a litter of pups, the dam a Sydney Silky terrier.

The puppies were just lovely and there was one black and tan just like his sire. I visited them every day and watched them grow. He was mine just a few weeks later. Months had passed and it was now autumn, I had been given a bicycle the previous Christmas which was my escape from reality, it enabled me to go further afield, the dog rode in the basket between the handlebars and went everywhere with me. Father put up a running wire so I could tie him up and stop him from following me if it wasn't safe for him.

Late one afternoon father returned from work, the dog was on his running chain and rushed to greet him, excited he got the chain tangled around father's legs, father picked the small dog up and threw him against the wall of the house, I rushed outside when the dog screamed in pain to comfort him, father went inside without a word, mother cleaned his grazed shins, then came out to find me sitting crying, holding my now whimpering dog. It was obvious he was badly hurt, she gently placed him on a blanket then into a box, we carried him inside and put him by the kitchen stove where it was warm. She gave him ½ an aspirin and he settled. Next morning he was up but carrying his back leg, he never walked on all 4 paws again, after a time he could put the hind leg down but could never put his full weight on it.

There were no vets practicing in small country towns, so we just had to nurse him till he got better with time. My view of my father was changed that night, and I never saw him the same way again, I think it shattered my innocence, there was no explanation, how could he have done what he did to a small creature who was just happy to see him, I couldn't understand it, but we never spoke of it.

Toodyay, my first home town in Western Australia, I still have fond memories of it.

> *The original townsite of Toodyay was determined in 1836, The current town of Toodyay was not always known by that name, initially Toodyay was located in what is now west Toodyay, some 5 km from its current location, repeated flooding caused the town centre to migrate to the area around the Newcastle convict depot, creating the town of Newcastle in 1860, after around 50 years of confusion, between the same named towns in Western Australia and New South Wales, the name of Newcastle was officially changed to Toodyay in 1910 and the original site became West Toodyay. The town is built adjacent to the floodplain of the Avon River, flooding of the river continued.*

In 1955 the river flooded the town again effectively cutting it in two when the Newcastle Bridge became submerged, lots of buildings were inundated and there was significant infrastructure damage.

For me it was a most awe-inspiring experience, not being aware of the cost to the community but observing first-hand the power of nature and what changes it could bring.

The main street of Toodyay was the high street, all the businesses had their shops along it, the butcher had a large ceramic pig wearing a blue sash with a rosette in the window, looking in from the street you could watch him make chops with his cleaver on a large log covered in flour. Sides of mutton, pork and quarters of beef hung on hooks along a rail, mince-meat and sausages, chops and steaks were laid out on trays behind a glass fronted counter, he wore a blue striped apron and the floor was covered in sawdust. There were 3 hotels, the town hall and shire office, a pharmacy which I loved to go into as there were large glass jars along the back wall with all manner of lotions, pills and potions. Medication was dispensed into little brown glass bottles with hand written labels and a plug of cotton-wool put under the stopper. To me it was very exotic.

The pharmacy also had a glass cabinet containing fine porcelain ornaments, crystal and silverware. I spotted a little ballerina that rotated on a stand. She wore a skirt of lace that had been dipped in porcelain. I badly wanted to give it to mother for her birthday. I had saved my pocket money, like other children I collected drink bottles and returned them to the store for a refund, this added to my kitty, I asked the pharmacist if I could buy the figurine and continue to pay for it bit by bit. He agreed, then he must have told father what I'd arranged. Father was furious, I received a dreadful dressing down on what the protocol was, that children were not allowed to do as elders did. I certainly knew my place afterwards. He redeemed the figurine; I didn't get any more pocket money until the debt was settled. Then I was permitted to give it to mother. She treasured it for the rest of her life, I have it now.

The general store was equally interesting, the majority of goods were in large bags, boxes or barrels and weighed out on scales, then wrapped in brown paper and tied with string or put into white or brown paper bags, broken biscuits especially were a treat, the pieces making a lovely variety, sweets in glass jars counted out and put into little waxed paper bags, the shelves along the back wall loaded with cans and packets with coloured labels. On the other side of the store was the hardware and homewares section. Upstairs was the drapery, linens and haberdashery, big bolts of cloth, blankets and all the notions you can imagine were available there. Mother often purchased items on the Lay-by system, this is where I had got the idea from to buy the figurine. However, there wasn't any real roasted coffee to be had during that time in country Australia, people drank a coffee substitute, coffee and chicory essence, a most foul-tasting concoction which upset mother very much as coffee was something she missed terribly.

Our '*Oma*' sent parcels from Germany, for our birthdays and Christmas, full of continental wonders, coffee, chocolate, marzipan and gingerbread, as well as toys and story books, these were so eagerly awaited and gratefully received, as were her letters written on the finest tissue paper a single page that was folded into an 'air mail' envelope.

I was a regular visitor to a farm on the edge of town, Mrs Kelly who lived there had invited me into her world of vegetable gardens, orchards and farm animals. Showed me how to care for them, I loved feeding lambs and chickens. She showed me how to make banana pudding with chilled evaporated milk, we baked scones and she made sponge cakes as soft as clouds. Often, I just made it home before dark. We had lots of great times living in this little country town, sleeping under the stars on hot summer nights, swimming in the river with gilgies nibbling our toes and leeches stuck to our legs. Uncle taught me to swim, then laughed at my amateur style of paddling around, swimming 'dog-paddle' like my dog was much easier. Floating in an inflated car tube looking up at the clouds was quite special.

My second little dog didn't get to have a long life. One day while out mushrooming with me, he picked up a fox bait, that evening he was very sick, strychnine poisoning is a hard death. Father had recently taken up hunting and went to get his rifle, that night everyone cried. Then more bad news, the tannin factory was shutting down. Father had to get another job, he found work at the TB Sanatorium at Wooroloo, it was to be a stopgap until he found the work he was used to. Living apart from family is lonely so he adopted a rescue dog, a wire-haired terrier, for company.

I'd been a relatively healthy child, apart from the usual childhood ailments, but my luck ran out at Halloween 1958. I was knocked off my bike by a car, my lovely bike ruined, my skull fractured, a deep cut to the back of my head and gravel rash down my face, arm and leg. I was concussed, mother picked me up off the road, our neighbour took care of Barbara, the ambulance took us to Northam Hospital, excruciating headaches followed, I was kept in a darkened room with no pillow, not able to sit up. I remember peeping out of the window to see the fireworks on Guy Faulks night, then being sedated as I was so ill. Four weeks later I was allowed home, summer was ruined, no swimming, tennis, or reading, vision in my right eye still blurred. I had a miserable convalescence. Mother taught me embroidery and some fancy sewing techniques like smocking and hemstitching to pass the time.

Father had found another job, however it was down at Northcliffe in the south of the State, so considerable upheaval and relocation of our family ensued. There was Barbara's cat, a lovely ginger and white tom to rehome, it wasn't considered possible to take him with us! He was taken to Mrs. Kelly's farm, she said one more would make no difference, he beat us back home. We had to leave him behind but our near neighbour the railway station master's wife, said she'd take care of him and eventually he'd come and live with her. Our chickens were also in peril, the young ones were given away, the old hens weren't wanted, considered boilers only good for soup, and then there was our rooster Karl, a magnificent Black Australorp, none of us could eat our dinner that night, or roast chicken for a very long time. Barbara hasn't eaten it since, mother didn't make chicken soup for years.

* * *

Northcliffe

The household was packed up and everything loaded onto the train. Necessities packed in the car, goodbyes said and off to Northcliffe we drove. It seemed to take an eternity, the countryside changed as we left farmlands behind, down the Darling Escarpment to the coastal plain and then south into the big timber country. Father's job was at the sawmill. We stayed at the Northcliffe Hotel until our furniture and household effects arrived, then moved into our allocated house out at Milltown. "Deliverance Country" is the name that comes to mind now, only we didn't know the name back then.

Living among strangers in an unfamiliar community, we were the outsiders, the foreigners once again. For me it was daunting, Barbara fitted right in, she was accepted and loved by everyone, roamed about with all the other kids her age. The house was enormous, our furniture only filled half of it, the other rooms were closed up. Tall trees, giant black kangaroo paws, a whole range of different wildflowers, tree ferns, even the flora was unfamiliar. We were enrolled to start school, there may have been a school bus but we elected to walk through the forest and pick blackberries on the way to and from school, late for class most days.

One weekend father decided to take us to Windy Harbour, that was a feat in itself, no made road, just a sand track lined with planks, he was told to stay on the planks, "don't get bogged in the sand, there's no guarantee of help to get you out", four-wheel drive vehicles not in common usage back then. Father thought we had run over a snake, he'd been told if that happened, they could get trapped under the vehicle, a scary thought, fortunately it hadn't happened. The sand was soft and the snake must have escaped. When we got there, it was beautiful, wild and windy, the Point D'Entrecasteaux national park is spectacular. Well worth the effort but definitely not a swimming beach for little girls.

Towards the end of summer there was a bad fire, we were cut off from Milltown being at school, so the timber company covered trucks in wet tarpaulins and we were loaded into these and taken home through thick smoke and flying embers. We thought of it as a big adventure, weren't the least bit frightened, unlike the parents of Milltown who wanted their children home and safe. The fire burnt out overnight, school was closed for the rest of the week. When it reopened, we discovered all our blackberries had been burnt, just blackened canes and the odd smoldering logs remained along our track.

There were other delights though, passion fruit hanging over back fences, strawberry patches, people had vegetable gardens, some growing giant rhubarb stems. I was banned from the local swimming hole by the other kids, because of my dog - my shadow, he was just too protective; he bit or tried to bite everyone including mother, although he never tried to bite Barbara or father, father's rescue dog had become MY dog, he went everywhere with me. We also acquired two kittens; Barbara always found kittens that needed a home.

It was a very harsh winter, dreadfully cold and wet. The dog was meant to sleep out in the woodshed, it was so cold he barked, so I smuggled him into our bedroom and he slept under my bed, mother must have known, but said nothing as he was always back in the shed by breakfast. She had the good sense not to come into our room in the mornings, just called us through the door. Mother became very ill that winter, bronchitis had turned to pleurisy, then pneumonia. Complications of the 'flu, she had to go into hospital in Pemberton. I had to grow up, assume responsibility. Father was working shifts so it was up to me to get us up and ready for school. This didn't sit well with Barbara; she didn't approve of the change in hierarchy and besides it was nice and warm in bed. I had to enlist the help of our next-door neighbour so that we did get to school.

Before he went to work father would chain the dog up in the woodshed, one afternoon, when he got home, it was to a commotion in the lane behind our house, our neighbour had shot himself, he had also shot and killed our little dog. Years later I learnt through mother telling me the story, that he'd had a drinking problem and his family were subjected to domestic violence. The back lane was cordoned off and became taboo, making it a more desirable and curious place to visit. His wife and children moved away soon afterward. Barbara and I continued to raid the strawberry patch.

Our parents were disappointed with the move and conditions in Northcliffe, so when father found work in North Fremantle we packed up and moved again. Firstly, to a rental house in North Cottesloe, Barbara and I had to attend North Cottesloe Primary School for term 3, a completely loathsome time for both of us. I don't think mother liked living there either, then we moved into a shop which had been converted into a house in South Fremantle.

* * *

Fremantle

We had come to my happy place, Barbara loved it there as well, by the beach, the Fishing Boat Harbour and the Esplanade. Fremantle, so exotic and cosmopolitan, such fun to explore, so many lovely people. The corner store at the top of our street was an Aladdin's Cave, sacks with the tops rolled down, boxes and barrels of anchovies, sundried tomatoes, olives of every colour, beans of endless varieties. Colourful cans of olive oil, jars of pickled vegetables and always sweets and delicacies on the counter, the smell of roasted coffee beans. The shop was run by a generous 'grandfatherly' man, he was so kind, everyone loved him. Barbara was a frequent shopper, buying sweets on credit with the promise of paying tomorrow, she never left empty handed.

From the cereal factory where he was working, father brought home a full set of collectables for us, clear tinted plastic animals of various colours, which were the tokens in the cereal boxes, the incentive for mothers to buy that brand of cereal. Barbara peddled them door to door, 1 penny for the small ones, 3 pence for the larger ones, a very enterprising little girl. Everyone loved her so applauded her initiative and purchased her wares. I found a lovely gold wristwatch on a demolition site among the rubble, mother had it serviced for me by friends, watchmakers who had come to Australia on the same ship as us, then settled in Fremantle establishing their business, a jewellery shop on South Terrace.

Every door in the street was open to the children, the families who lived in this street were like one big family. The baker came with a horse and cart loaded with the most amazing crusty bread, the greengrocer came with his wagon of fresh fruit and vegetables, both occasions for the women to gather in the street to chat while inspecting the wares, before making their purchase. Mother hated the way the women would squeeze the loaves to check that they weren't hollow, and smell the tomatoes to ensure they were properly ripened. The milkman delivered bottles of milk in the early hours of the morning, it was an evening chore to put the empty bottles on the door step, the number put out the indication of how many he should leave, sometimes mother put a rolled note into a bottle, the order for a small bottle of cream to be left also. Payment for the milk would be made by putting the cash into an envelope and placing it under one of the bottles for the milkman to collect during the delivery round.

This was the heart of the fishing community in South Fremantle. Also, home to the waterfront workers who worked on the docks of Fremantle Harbour and their families, a wonderful mix of humanity. That part of Fremantle wasn't just residential, there were warehouses, wool stores and various other enterprises conducting businesses, across the street was a bottle yard, a recycling depot, there was a high brick wall with glass shards embedded on top, double wrought iron gates faced the street. The wall was excellent to practice tennis against, a line drawn to indicate the net height, a ball tied to a brick with a long strand of elastic, I could practice my forehand and backhand strokes for hours.

We lived here for my last year of primary school at South Terrace Primary. I didn't like that school very much, that's actually an understatement, I disliked it intensely. The corporal punishment inflicted on classmates was just plain wrong, the cane surely belonged in the past. Young boys, especially high-spirited ones, didn't deserve to have fat old men beating them so cruelly. The constant mispronunciation of my name still galled me, on the enrolment form my full name had been entered, they started to call me Angelina, the Italian version of my name, the head teacher embarrassed me in front of the assembly - so I couldn't sing in tune, easy solution - just don't put me in the choir, there was no need to make a public spectacle of me. I got to play in the netball team but wasn't good at athletics.

Barbara attended the same school, in the Alma Street building. At the end of year celebration, she wore a pink fairy costume which mother had made for her, she looked every inch the part. I made a few friends but the friendships didn't last beyond that year. I spent a lot of time hitting that tennis ball, dreaming of becoming a champion one day, or at the beach. We were often present at the bay when fishermen were casting nets for bait fish, there were always some left for us to collect, mother would prepare them for our dinner, freshly fried sardines on crusty bread are a true treat.

I loved the Fremantle Markets, such an enchanting place, derelict at the time with lots of cats living there, being fed by a strange looking old lady nightly. Attending the Presbyterian Youth Club, celebrating Halloween, Girl Guides, learning skills like knot tying just to get another badge. Such a wonderful city to explore and get to know every nook, cranny and back alley. I loved watching the ships and tug boats coming into port and fishing boats coming into the harbour. I played tennis at the club and went to watch the football at Fremantle Oval. Father started by working at a cereal factory in North Fremantle, but the pull of the ocean was too strong, it had him on the fishing boats by the end of that year.

Our parents had been on the State Housing list for some time, their name came up, a house was available. We inspected three homes, one in Hilton Park, two in Hamilton Hill, all brand new. Mother chose the cottage set across a corner block, it had a blue tile roof, walls clad in asbestos sheeting, I often wondered why she didn't pick the cream brick one across the street, it was on a corner as well and sat straight, parallel to the street. The suburb of Hamilton Hill was too far away from the Fremantle I had come to know and love; I wasn't as happy as they were to be moving.

By the time I was 13 years old I had certainly experienced quite a number of changes. Australia too had not stood still and was changing:

- Holden cars were being manufactured here.
- Australia had become a signatory to the Universal Declaration of Human Rights.
- Construction of the Snowy Mountains Hydro-Electric Scheme had begun.
- Troops were sent to South Korea to assist in the Korean War, wool prices boomed as a result.
- The Menzies Government held a referendum to Ban the Communist Party, which was rejected.
- The ANZUS Treaty was signed.
- Nuclear testing had begun off the coast of Western Australia.
- There'd been a Royal visit by Queen Elizabeth II and Prince Phillip in 1954.
- Melbourne hosted the Olympic Games in 1956.
- Rock-n-Roll was making an impression, Johnny O'Keefe reached number 1 on the charts with the song "Wild One". Slim Dusty attained international success with his song "The Pub with No Beer".
- Construction of the Sydney Opera House began.
- Myxomatosis was released to control the rabbit plague.

* * *

My Teenage Years

Looking back now; the parent's dream of a home of their own being realised, was actually an unsettling time for me, I wasn't very happy for most of the years I lived there, maybe it was due to adolescence, or the sense that the family dynamic was about to change.

We moved to Hamilton Hill. Mother was happy she finally had that place that she could call home, a place of her own, no more rent or landlords. One day it would belong to her outright. Father went from one boat to the next. His luck didn't hold, the catch was confiscated, or there were problems here there and everywhere. He was paid in fish and crayfish, he sold some of it privately. Mother arranged for the seafood to be kept in the chiller at our local butcher shop, she swapped crayfish for mincemeat and chops, fish cutlets for anything the butcher would give, gravy beef or stewing steak, cheap cuts of pork, lamb or beef. Mother got very inventive in using crayfish, cooking it in so many different ways. Barbara and I swapped crayfish sandwiches at school for jam, peanut butter or vegemite. Our 'plate' at events was always popular, no one else brought platters of crayfish salad or bowls of mornay. To this day neither of us can eat it, we don't enjoy fish either for that matter. It still sticks in our throats.

Father and I often spent hours walking along the beach chatting, sometimes on stormy winters days, heads bent low against the wind. He'd tell me of his ambitions for the future. I was curious to know more about him, especially his childhood, about his family and how he had met my mother, reluctantly answering my barrage of questions. He eventually started to talk about his youth, the war years, his naval service and how he met my mother. This is his story.

He was the only child of Paul Richard Hoffmann and Irma Leonie Hoffmann nee Wiedemann, born on the 29th May 1921 in Berlin-Charlottenburg, Germany. His father was engaged in the timber industry; had forest leases and contracts mainly supplying poles to the government for telegraph and electricity. They had a country house near Danzig but mostly lived in their Berlin city apartment. His mother was a socialite and spent a lot of her time playing bridge. He told me that he'd had a governess looking after him as a child. His favourite sporting activity was cycling. He was educated at a Private College and graduated attaining the *Abitur* or Leaving Certificate, matriculated to study at the Technical University in Berlin at the faculty of Marine Engineers.

However, against his parent's wishes he applied to enter the Naval Academy in Schleswig-Holstein, he was unsuccessful for various reasons, he'd had Rheumatic fever as a child, an inflammatory disease that has the potential to lead to heart damage and he had an astigmatism in one eye. He wasn't a German Citizen, his father being a citizen of the Danzig Free State. A city at the mouth of the Vistula River on the Baltic Sea and once the capital of West Prussia, historically headquarters of the Hanseatic League. In the spring of 1939 tensions were mounting over Poland's rejection of the German claims to Danzig, the old HANSA seaport, that had been made a Free City by the treaty of Versailles. The family fortunes took a dramatic downturn, his father's leases were terminated and the country house resumed. His father died of cancer in Berlin in 1943.

Early in 1940, shortly after the beginning of WWII father volunteered to join the German Navy, sailing on the minesweeper "M1" for several years, his duties were in the engine room as a 'stoker'.

The "M1" minesweeper nick-named "Tiger of the Fjords" was commissioned in 1938, first used to ferry naval infantry to the battleship "Schleswig-Holstein" in preparation for the Polish campaign and was involved in this once war began, at the end of this campaign she was relocated to the North Sea. M1 was part of the naval component of Operation Siegfried, the occupation of the islands of Dago, Osel and Moon of Estonia. Later she operated in the Norwegian and North Seas, based in Norway. In April 1944 Eberhard Kuhn took command, in January 1945 she was attacked and sunk by a direct hit from 'Tallboy' bombs dropped by Lancaster bombers of the RAF, in Nordbyfjord approx. 40 km from Bergen, Norway. 20 of the crew of 34 were killed in the sinking. Her wreckage sank to a depth of 340 meters. Father was on watch at the time not below decks and said this is why he survived the sinking.

The captain was honoured with the '*Ritterkreuz*" the highest order of merit, all the crew members were decorated with the "Iron Cross first class" in recognition of their bravery. Naturally he was very proud of this; he also had a book written by the captain titled "Tigerflag ahead". He kept this in a brass box along with his whistle and lanyard, and the tallies, the black silk ribbons inscribed with the names of the ships he served on. I loved looking at the photos in the book, especially the picture of the cat and always imagined that it would have survived because of the nine lives myth. Unfortunately, these mementos are all lost now.

He was rescued after having been submerged in the icy waters for several hours, suffering hypothermia and had sustained minor injuries to his feet. After his recovery he sailed on the minesweeper 'M2" until surrendering at the end of the war. He was a prisoner of war in Denmark, after being released to Hamburg he made contact with the union and found work at the wharf.

Bowing to his mother's wishes he returned to Berlin in early 1946 and registered at an employment office, was initially employed by the Allied Forces working as a labourer on demolition sites, it was hard physical work but it qualified him for better food rations. The Technical University Marine Engineers campus was out of bounds at this stage so he was unable to resume studying but his mother had managed to get him enrolled at an Interpreter College; after graduating he was employed by the British occupation forces as an interpreter and driver for their personnel.

He had been introduced to my mother while home on leave by mutual friends in 1940; they had dated for a couple of years then lost contact. After the war ended, they bumped into each other again outside the employment office where he was registering on his return to

Berlin and resumed their relationship. On the 28th September 1946 he married my mother.

During these times together, when he'd told me about his youth, we'd also explore the stock in used car lots, he with dreams in his eyes. One day he hoped to have a nice car. He was always restless; we had no sooner settled at Hamilton Hill when he wanted to upgrade to a more prestigious home in Applecross, that didn't eventuate. Next; he wanted to invest in land in the new area of Medina or Orelia, would spend Sunday afternoon driving around looking at lots. Mother often refused to accompany him, knowing that these were 'pipe dreams', they were barely making ends meet. If she hadn't found work, as distasteful as it was to her, the situation would have been even leaner. One winter my sister and I needed new coats as we had outgrown ours. She undid all the seams of her own coat, washed and pressed the fabric, then re-cut it using the reverse side and re-made it for me. I emulated this unpicking the seams of mine, so that she could make a coat for Barbara.

I went out on the boats with father whenever I could. One particular trip to an unfamiliar fishing ground, the craypots came up with a good catch, then a strange process began. The crays were scrubbed clean of a yellow substance which was adhered to their underside before being packed and put into the chiller. I wondered why they were doing this. The answers came soon enough. The whole catch was confiscated by the fisheries inspector and the company heavily fined. No wages on that trip, they had broken the law! These were female crays full of eggs ready to spawn. Mostly undersize into the bargain. Stupid greed had cost dearly and threatened the future of the industry. We found out later that one of the crew had tipped off the inspectors to alert them to what was happening on that boat.

Father went from the fishing fleet to a hydrographic survey ship, they surveyed for the ports of Weipa in North Queensland and Barrow Island in Western Australia, amongst others. The company was based on the east coast, we saw less and less of father. Mother was working at all sorts of menial jobs, taking in sewing, cleaning, assembly line packing, whatever she could get. With father away mother kept us a family, dressed us beautifully and maintained discipline, ensured we ate well and were healthy. Supervised homework to make sure we did well at school. Kept the house clean and had a lovely garden. We helped doing chores, it was only fair, it taught us responsibility and gave us skills, our routine gave us stability, she took us to the beach in summer, taught us about the arts, music and literature, history and culture, manners, protocol and appropriate behaviour. Phone calls from a call box with a stack of coins to talk to father was a treat, but mainly it was letter writing and waiting for the mail.

Barbara was enrolled at the local convent school in Hilton Park, although the State primary school was at the top of our street. I started at high school, there wasn't one in Hamilton Hill or in any of the surrounding areas so I was enrolled at John Curtin Senior High School in Fremantle. It was a relatively new establishment but due to the big area it drew students from it was really too small from the outset. Year 8 students attended the Annexe, Princess May, formerly Princess May High School for Girls, now it was co-ed. An antiquated freezing cold in winter, stiflingly hot in summer, formidable stone edifice, it looked haunted. Once a week we got to walk to the top of the hill and attend JCSH for a single subject: Domestic Science! For girls only. Term one - Laundry, Term two – Sewing, Term three – Cooking.

Boys got to do woodwork and metalwork. Gender roles were set in stone. From my perspective, there wasn't much to like about high school, the outside world was changing and the education system was stuck firmly in Victorian times, and so was the attitude of the teaching staff. The curriculum set in stone as hard as the stuff Princess May School was built from.

I was the odd one out all over again; the foreign girl resurfaced; my uniforms were home made with love but made me stand out as different. I desperately wanted to blend in, my sports tunic was too short so I spent most sports sessions sitting on the bench, not permitted to participate. I only had a 2-piece swim-suit so wasn't allowed to get into the water, it was so humiliating. My pullover was hand knitted, mother had made my tunic and blouses out of a different fabric to the custom-made uniforms that everyone else had. My beret wasn't soft and floppy, it had a firm stitched band so it lived in the bottom of my schoolbag!

Year 9 was better, we had new neighbours, a family from Victoria. A naval officer, posted to the training academy at HMAS Leeuwin for Naval Cadets. Our families soon became good friends. I now had a girlfriend and we went to the same school, because of her father's job we also got to go to the Friday night chaperoned dances at Leeuwin and have fun. Her house was fun to go to as well, we were allowed to play teen music, watch TV music shows, eat junk food and drink soft drinks, none of which was permitted at our house. Her mother curled our hair with a curling iron, big hair was in vogue, we back-combed (teased) our hair to get volume and started to wear it up in 'Beehives or French rolls' feeling so very grown up. At school we had to have it tied back into a ponytail or plaits.

Academically you could say I was average, better at some subjects, hopeless at math. Father arranged for me to go to night classes at the Technical College for math tutoring, I went to art classes instead, my pen and ink drawings giving my secret away, not attending math tutoring didn't improve my grades.

I played tennis in summer, the club hosted social activities for teens, adolescence suddenly became fun. My winter sport was hockey, it was a long way to Fremantle for training and most games seemed to be away games, so there were lots of bus and train trips involved. I hated umpiring when we had a bye, the parents on the side-lines were so judgemental and critical. My pocket money was earned doing chores and in rather short supply so lots of times it was walk and run a number of stops to save on fares. I was fit in those days though.

Year 10 was much the same at school, home life rocky, corporal punishment wasn't unknown either, "children should be seen not heard" was a house rule. One evening on the now rare occasions father was at home, our parents were in the living room watching the news on TV, my sister and I were in the kitchen folding the washing, chatting and fooling about. Suddenly the door was flung open and father stormed into the room raging that we were making too much noise, when I protested, he hit the side of my head so hard that I was propelled across the length of the room hitting my head against the refrigerator, stunned, sliding to the floor. The next thing I remember was mother standing over me, helping me to my feet and guiding me to my room so I could lay down. That was the last time he raised a hand to me; mother was also quite free with a slap and the 'spare the rod and spoil the child' rule was part of her parenting approach.

As I've already said; father had had too many misadventures during his time on the fishing boats, money was always short. There was added financial pressure now, living apart meant that father had personal expenses to meet, in addition to sending money to us. Mother worked nights at a sports shoe factory packing shoes for shipment, during the day she worked at cleaning jobs to help make ends meet. Father's eventual leaving the fishing industry to work on a hydrographic survey ship, led to increased time away from home and mother was left to take charge. This caused tension between us, her rules were hard to adhere to, if I went to the library after school and caught a later bus home, she would be so angry with me it often had me in tears, she could be so unreasonable. If she was working on a particular day, I was expected to start dinner which I didn't mind, she would leave a list of what I needed to do. I enjoyed cooking but didn't like cleaning or ironing which were my weekend chores. At the end of the school year, in the lead up to Christmas I got a casual job, in a department store toy department, the job lasted 4 weeks. Finally, a pay check, the princely sum of £4, 10s, 6d, per week, about $8.55 in today's money, however the purchasing power was far greater in 1962.

At the end of Year 10 after successfully passing my Junior Certificate and with tertiary education not an option, (father not seeing a need for higher education for his daughter) school days were behind me. It was time to consider my future. I had suggested that studying horticulture was appealing, my tennis coach who was also a family friend was a greenkeeper, he had told me quite a lot about his profession, this was considered entirely inappropriate, such an apprenticeship completely unseemly, a male domain. A newspaper cadetship was laughed at, what could I possibly hope to contribute, so becoming a journalist was also out of the question. Kindergarten teaching was unattainable as there was to be no Leaving Certificate or Matriculation for me. Most other lines of work suitable for a young lady didn't appeal to me, so I settled on a career in nursing.

While I was waiting to apply for the next intake at a training hospital, mother insisted I attend Business College and get office experience, something to always fall back on she said. I graduated from Business College; my first position was with a family-owned firm who had a shoe agency. The office premises were in the back rooms of a very dark and some-what dingy inner-city hotel, the previous accommodation part having been turned into commercial office spaces. Manufacturers of ladies' fashion shoes would send a seasonal sample range to the agency; these samples were arranged on long tables in what had once been a ballroom, when the new season range display was ready, the various shoe stores would send their buyers to view the range, then place their orders, when the stock arrived my boss would deliver it to the various stores. If a particular style proved popular then more stock would be ordered and delivered the same way. He would also on occasion take samples of men's shoes out to the stores as these didn't have the same appeal to warrant a display. My position was temporary, lasting for six months. When my tenure was over; I was presented with a pair of shoes, one size 7 the other size $7^{1/2}$. I had to stuff wadding into the toe in order to wear them. Did someone pack them in error! Or was he aware and gifting me a pair of odd shoes?

Milestone; I had learnt to drive and was allowed to borrow the family car now and then. Freedom to go out with friends, to the beach and to pool parties and dances with people my age, loud music and fun without parental supervision. It was a summer of surf, fun and light-heartedness. On New Year's Eve, I'd been out surfing with friends and a wave knocked the board into my face splitting my lip. That night at the cabaret dressed in my new dress I was sporting a fat lip, it was the first time I'd been allowed to attend a New Year's Eve party with the adults, when we got home my little sister was quite tipsy, she had drunk mother's pineapple and white wine spritzer.

My next position was in the office of a mechanical repair workshop, they did motor vehicle servicing, panel beating and engine reconditioning. They also sold prime movers, there was a showroom for their heavy vehicle display. My duties were receptionist-telephonist, and assistant to the accountant. I was also the 'tea lady' and needed to dust the showroom and trucks. A friend I'd met at business college had meanwhile got a job at a dental practice and switched careers becoming a dental nurse. From what she told me it sounded more interesting than what I was doing.

When the opportunity arose for training at the Perth Dental Hospital I applied and got a position, unfortunately this didn't work out, the matron heard that father wanted the family to move to Victoria where his ship was based, although nothing was confirmed I was asked to resign. The reason given, Matron had decreed that my spot should go to someone who was more likely to stay and complete the training. The notion that I could actually live independently and stay in WA never occurred to anyone, and I was severely reprimanded when I suggested it at home. So, I went to work at another firm's office, again as receptionist-telephonist. Ultimately; I was the one to relocate.

My next job was at a flour mill in North Cottesloe, an awkward place to get to. It was between stops on both bus or rail routes, so entailed a considerable walk no matter which stop or transport I used.

It also required a change in Fremantle as the bus from Hamilton Hill went into Fremantle or Perth via the Canning Highway, North Cottesloe being on the Stirling Highway. I befriended a girl working at the mill in the laboratory, we shared the same lunchbreak time and met in the lunchroom. She had a far different upbringing to myself, being a descendant of one of the old pioneer families from the Busselton area, she had attended a private girls' college, whilst I had gone to a State high school. This didn't matter to either of us, we had a lot of fun together, visiting her family farm and spending time on the beaches in the Busselton area. She invited me to go to a function with her, the launch of a new wine variety, at the premises of the Royal Commonwealth Society in Subiaco. As I was an unfamiliar face one of the dowagers made it her business to discover who I was, and where I came from. After learning my heritage, still the little foreign girl, she quickly reminded my friend that she should be more careful about who she brought to these types of functions. We had a good laugh about this and left with a bottle of the wine each under our coats.

When I started to earn a wage, I paid mother a percentage of my wages for board and lodging, she saved this money and when I left home to go out on my own, she had a bankroll saved for me, she taught me how to budget, for bus fares, fuel for the car, saving towards new clothes, money for grooming, all valuable lessons. I was still eager to pursue a nursing career and had applied at all the training hospitals in the Perth and Fremantle areas. Mother saw an advertisement in the paper for student nurses in Darwin, the pay much higher due to the tropical and taxation zone allowances than local trainees, a live-in position with quarters adjacent to the hospital. I passed the entrance test and interview and was accepted for the next intake due in March 1965. I gave notice at work, they were shocked, told me that female staff only left the firm to get married. I purchased a matching set of suitcases on lay-by. I really was about to fly the coop and become ME.

The situation at home was unchanged. Mother was obviously feeling the stress of being a sole parent and her moods were extremely unpredictable, one afternoon on returning home from work I found every single one of my belongings in a heap on the front lawn, she had thrown it all out the window, my bedroom was bare. She had even broken some of the items I treasured like the ivory handles of my manicure set and the pretty hairbrush, comb and vanity mirror. I was utterly confused as to what brought on this level of rage, was she so keen to be rid of me that she couldn't wait for my departure date to Darwin or what was the issue? I never found out, just tossed everything back into my room, climbed in through the window and spent the evening sorting and restoring order. Upset that she felt she needed to act this way and that she had broken my things, some of which had been gifts from my grandmother. When I finally faced her, she acted as if everything was fine, didn't mention that anything had triggered her extreme behaviour.

With mother so very unhappy and working hard at menial jobs; father away for long periods, I was really looking forward to my great escape. The thought of leaving my lovely sister behind was heartbreaking and I wondered how she would cope, especially with mother's moods, however the excitement of getting away overrode everything.

Much was changing in the world:

- The space race was well and truly underway.
- Perth was hosting the Empire Games (now the Commonwealth Games).
- The shock wave of JFK's assassination still reverberated.
- Vietnam was at war and conscription loomed large in Australia.
- Music was front and centre, brilliant new bands making their mark and new dance crazes were a thing.

Darwin here I come.

3

Darwin - Northern Territory

My first flight was with MMA airways, it took hours with many landings and take-offs. Hello Rhonda, a fellow trainee nurse from Perth, my first room-mate. The humidity when we landed was like a wet wall, welcome to Darwin during the wet season.

My introduction to the hospital and life in the 1960s wasn't quite as free as the era has been portrayed, it may have been in some parts of the world but not where I was, institutionalised is a better description, not a lot different to boarding school. Curfews, group housing, shift work, lectures, communal dining with fixed meal times, room inspections, roll call by the night-sister patrol at 10.30 pm. We needed to be in or questions would be asked. Our reason for non-compliance had better be a good one or there would be consequences. I'd turned 18, though still not an adult in the eyes of the law. After being in Darwin for a couple of months I was getting used to the routine, the responsibilities of working in a hospital, the shift work, seeing human suffering and learning to really care, developing empathy, learning the social skills of living in a share house and making friends with fellow students from around Australia.

Organised social activities were the norm, the RAAF and Navy bases had lots of young men, so did the police barracks. Nurses were sought-after guests for 'chaperoned' dances, picnics and barbecues. It felt a little like we were being displayed at a meat market. Graduate sisters were introduced to the officers, trainee nurses to the enlisted men. Did we need these minders to control our lives, taking over from parents, or was it yet another hangover from the Victorian era, silly girls needing to be managed? Swimming in the ocean during the wet season wasn't a good idea, there are nasty stingers in tropical waters, box jellyfish and Portuguese Man'o War with very long stinging tentacles. The local pool or freshwater springs was where we went, I contracted 'tropical ear', a very painful condition. I learnt to waterski, loved the feeling of freedom racing across the water, had a fall crossing the wake of a boat and hurt my knee. Life isn't without risk.

The climate was so different from where I grew up in Western Australia, the humidity was sapping, we needed to change our uniforms half way through our eight-hour shift, everything felt damp, our hair was lank, leather goods turned mouldy, mould even grew on walls, but our enthusiasm remained undaunted. We were told "the 'Dry' season is paradise". On days off we swam, played tennis and squash, took picnic lunches out to parks, the botanic gardens were fabulous, we ate cuisine from different cultures, met so many different people. One of our patients was from a ship with a Chinese crew, when the man recovered and returned to the ship, a fellow nurse and I were formally invited to come and dine on the ship by the captain, after a long lecture from matron we were allowed to attend. I can say that we were overwhelmed by the hospitality, with the most amazing meal of exotic dishes being presented to us, there was an interpreter present who explained every dish to us and the order in which it was customary to eat the food. It truly was a memorable evening.

Communicating with home required letter writing, I was lax in that department and having fun, phone calls needed to be pre-booked through the hospital switch and were expensive. I guess I failed in the letter writing department, the family was unhappy with my lack of effort. Mother sent me a postcard with only her address on it, as a not-so-subtle reminder that she'd like to hear from me occasionally.

The year was drawing to a close. The build-up to the wet season had begun, this was my first Christmas away from home, I was on duty on Christmas Day and had no expectation of any celebration. What a surprise, the hospital put on an amazing feast in the dining room, it was decorated and festive, I may have felt homesick but not for long, this was another first for me. An Australian Christmas Dinner, so very different from the European celebration I had grown up with. Darwin; vibrant and exotic a melting pot. We matured quickly, discovered 'late night' at the pub, drank, danced and had fun, we learnt to fly, some of us soared, others stumbled or fell. Some girls got married, left to settle into family life. New intakes of girls arrived to start their nursing careers. Young men in uniform went to Vietnam, their girls cried as they said farewell.

First year exams over, I had passed. The stripe on my cap would change from red to green when the first annual leave was over, some of my friends were going to exotic places, Singapore, Dilli in East Timor, Kuala Lumpur in Malaysia, I was booked to go back to Perth, (to the same situation I'd left a year ago, parents pulling different ways, little sister growing up fast, why was I going back? It was the family's expectation! I aimed to please everyone but myself, is that weak or considerate? I tended to doubt myself, questioning, do I fit in, am I the square peg, lacking in self-confidence, always looking for approval and acceptance.

The break was neither pleasant nor memorable, mother had given away most of the things I had left behind, particularly upsetting was all my books, I now felt a stranger in the family home. She had plans to convert my bedroom into a formal dining room complete with a chandelier over the dining table. Barbara was pleased to see me; she was at high school now and was much more grown up. Father happened to be there, on learning that I had a cheque account as well as a savings account found it necessary to stress the importance of a balanced cheque book. He must have thought me to be extremely stupid, did he not consider that I may have picked up a few clues while at business college.

One afternoon as I was walking to the bus stop at the end of our street I came across a vehicle accident, a car had run into the telephone box, the driver was still behind the wheel but not responding, I checked on him and alerted a neighbour who phoned for an ambulance. Then I commenced first aid as we had been taught, the man regained consciousness which was fortunate for me, apart from a minor head wound he seemed unhurt but the smell of alcohol was overwhelming. I left the scene when the ambulance arrived. Apart from catching up with a few school friends there weren't any highlights. I was happy to be going back to Darwin. The girls who didn't go on overseas holidays, also went to visit their families, in South Australia, Victoria, New South Wales and Queensland, the only one who didn't come back was from South Australia.

When we returned to Darwin we were issued with our new caps, with the green stripe indicating second year trainee and were allocated different rooms and new roommates. Second year had begun, decimal currency was the new legal tender. Time wasn't standing still. Our training continued and our responsibilities grew. On some occasions the only staff for the late shift would be one duty sister and one or two trainees, I learnt a lot on those occasions. While working in one of the medical wards I was left to stay at the bedside of an extremely ill patient undertaking fifteen-minute observations, we didn't have electronic monitors back then, as the vital signs became alarming, I called for the duty sister, who called the doctor. Our patient didn't live to see the morning. Then I was instructed what to do to prepare the body for the last rites and the final farewell for the family. During my time working at the hospital this wasn't the only death I faced just the first, stillbirth, disease, accident, age, young and old are taken. The miracle of witnessing the recoveries of patients, of broken bodies being mended, then finally seeing them discharged back into the arms of family are what gave me the strength to want to go further ahead with my chosen career.

Collectively we nurses were looking at options for personal transport, one of the girls bought a red Mini Minor, another had a green Volkswagen, then a blue Vesper scooter appeared parked under the quarters. A scooter seemed ideal, several of us went to the Suzuki dealership and five of us left in a convoy of red and white scooters. We were mobile. I'd celebrated my 19th birthday, some of the girls were in serious relationships by then, more young men from the air force base were deploying to Vietnam, hearts were broken, others were into mere dalliances and played the field. I was in the latter group, a few casual dates but no-one to get serious with. No rush, I was building a career and looking to qualify, then to travel, just as so many of my generation were doing.

One evening as I came off shift and returned to our house there were two young men and two of the older nursing sisters sitting at the table of our common room, deep in conversation. One of the men caught my eye, I thought he was particularly nice looking, especially when he smiled. I asked one of the other girls if she knew who they were, she didn't know, just saying that she'd over-heard some of the conversation about horse riding and a rodeo at Katherine, and the sisters were going with them.

The dry season was here again. My shiny red scooter was my ticket to explore further afield, a friend from Victoria also had one, so did one of the girls who was a year ahead of us. We'd heard about Arnhem Land. Some of our patients had come to Darwin Hospital from remote settlements from there, we didn't really know how far it was or how to get there. The Northern Territory is a big place, I'd been to Katherine with a group of friends on a day trip and knew that there was a place called Rum Jungle, as one of the patients I'd nursed was from there. He was a geologist at the uranium mine, there was a township where the workers lived named Bachelor. There were a lot of bachelors in the Territory at the time, women were hugely outnumbered, perhaps the town was named for them, who knows?

Other places we'd visited down the Stuart Highway, Howard Springs, Humpty Doo, Adelaide River, where the war cemetery was, rows of white crosses, so solemn, the publican at the Adelaide River Hotel had a pony who had acquired a taste for beer, patrons thought it was fun to feed it, much to the detriment of the pony, he put on so much weight that he had to be relegated to a back paddock for his wellbeing. The Adelaide River is tidal, the water brackish, sharks frequently swam upriver to rid themselves of sea lice and sucker fish, it was also home to salt water crocodiles so not an ideal place to swim. Berri Springs, Daly River and Pine Creek, going with friends in cars none of it seemed that far away. I digress, my friends and I decided to go out to the Marrakai Plains to see if we could see any buffalo on our next lot of days off.

We filled our fuel tanks, packed a picnic into our saddle bags and took extra water bottles. The turn-off was at the 47-mile marker, Australia wasn't completely metric yet, still in change-over mode, one small oversight, we hadn't taken the isolation and distance into account in our eagerness to explore further afield, nor did we let anyone know what our plans were before heading south down the highway. A stupid mistake to make, but we didn't anticipate that anything could go awry.

Disaster was waiting for us just a little way along the track, flat tyres, not just one but two, our small tool kit wasn't much use at all. Out there on the plain there are crocodiles in the water holes, feral buffalo and pigs in considerable size herds, spiders, biting ants, flies, goannas and snakes; pythons and venomous snakes of varying sizes, just to name a few of the inhabitants. Night brings out the mosquitoes, big ones attacking like darts and sneaky little ones who hover like helicopters. From sandflies - there is no respite day or night. Our sensible older friend decided to go back to town, she was on nightshift so work started at midnight for her. We stayed with our scooters and waited, hoping for assistance, help to get us out of our predicament before dark. So, there we were, sitting on our immobile scooters in the blazing sun. I was still dressed in a leopard print bikini, clothes draped across the seat of my scooter, my friend had already changed back into her shorts and top after the short cooling swim we'd taken earlier at a creek some distance back. Then we heard a car engine, salvation, someone was coming; surely help was at hand.

Out of the mirage and dust came our rescue, "my knight in blue denim"- not on a charger but driving a dusty Falcon Ute. (His name, Mick Bailey, I was instantly smitten, Cupid's arrow struck hard.) The same young man I'd seen in the nurse's quarters not so very long ago, I recognised the sun-tan, flashing smile and sparkling eyes. He was wearing the afore mentioned blue jeans, a white shirt, RM Williams boots and a battered Akubra hat.

We were rescued. He lit a small fire and made us billy tea, then assessed our situation. The best idea seemed to be to load our scooters into the back of the Ute and continue on to his destination, Jimmy Creek Buffalo Abattoir. Along the way we learnt that his job was meat inspecting at the abattoir, he worked for the Northern Territory Administration, Animal Industries Branch. The abattoir was one of several that had been set up to control the population of feral buffalo. Their numbers, along with the feral pigs, causing much damage to the ecology of the top end of the Northern Territory, they were a disease threat to domestic herds, some carrying bovine tuberculosis. The buffalo hadn't been gazetted as livestock yet, so were the property of 'the Crown', under the control of the government who issued the permits for these abattoirs.

Some of these abattoirs were mobile and set up in various parts of what is now Kakadu National Park, like the one at Woolwonga Reserve[1] on the banks of 'Dreaming Waters'. Others such as Jimmy Creek were considered 'permanent' as they utilised previous 'camps' which usually began when early settlers tried to establish themselves on these vast plains. Some camps were rudimentary and used as bases for crocodile hunters or seasonal fishers. They mainly consisted of a corrugated iron hut and a few sheds or lean-tos. Jimmy Creek on Point Stuart pastoral lease was purpose built, an abattoir with a fully equipped machinery shed, the accommodation for the manager a corrugated iron clad small house, a Sidney Williams Hut.

---

[1] The Woolwonga – an Indigenous people of the Northern Territory were reputed to have been almost completely exterminated in the 1880s at Burrundie south of Darwin in reprisal for an incident in which some members of the tribe speared 4 miners. (Reference, Wikipedia – Wulwulam Article)

We were greeted by the manager, his wife and baby daughter. A young German couple seeking adventure and a better life; they reminded me a little of my parents. He was an adventurer looking for the last frontier, she looked lost, out of her depth and comfort zone, the baby a beautiful little girl, curly blond hair and blue eyes. They made us welcome; evening was approaching so repair to our scooters was put on hold till morning, we had no option but to stay the night. Fingers crossed our friend could explain our absence from our quarters.

I overheard the lady telling her husband in German that she had no spare rations to feed us all, wondering what she could do. They had no idea I was bi-lingual and understood what they were saying. I felt embarrassed, we didn't have much left in our saddlebags to contribute. I told Mick what she had said, he volunteered to make braised steak for everyone as there was plenty of meat in the chiller, and he had spuds and onions in his tucker box. Confusion on the young woman's face, what was this strange meal. Mick lit a fire outside on the ground, got a buffalo fillet from the chiller, sliced it, together with onions and potatoes. Then seared the meat in his camp-oven, sautéed the onions, seasoned with salt and pepper, added some water and tomato sauce, then laid the potato slices on top of the meat, lid on and the camp-oven sat in the coals. The young woman and I watched intently, she smiled and said "Ah! you fry it in water!", well not quite, we both learnt something new that evening. Mick then made 'johnny cakes', little individual dampers, cooked on a hotplate over the coals.

The meal was a great success, some of the workers from the abattoir joined us around the fire, and it was a most pleasant ending to the day. I had met someone special, eaten my first bush cooked camp-oven meal under the stars. Time for bed, our hosts had partitioned their hut with hessian and divided the space into 3 bedrooms, a living room and kitchen-dining area. We were shown into the middle bedroom, 2 shearer's beds under mosquito netting, my friend and I settled in for the night. What would tomorrow bring?

Mick was up before any of us, he had the fire stoked and a billy of tea made. Breakfast was left over johnny cakes with golden syrup. We went for a walk and he showed me around the complex explaining how the buffalo were field shot, loaded onto a trailer and brought into the abattoir, they had to be in for processing within the hour or would spoil and be condemned. His task to ensure the processing time line was met, to check the carcass for any sign of disease such as TB lesions and to ensure health standards and hygiene were maintained. The chilled meat was exported to Asia and Europe where game was popular. The meat deemed to be very healthy due to its low cholesterol fat content. Everyone working in the industry (except the inspector) was on contract and received payment at the end of the dry season, as the area wasn't accessible during the wet. Previously buffalo had been shot for hides and horns, crocodiles for hides.

I found some lovely plants growing down by the creek, popular house plants in southern regions. The jungle is full of surprises. Back at the workshop everyone was up and repairs to our tyres were done. After discussion, the manager decided to suspend operations for the day so that Mick could take us out to the highway with our scooters, not risking any more misadventures.

My friend and I said goodbye and thanked our hosts. When we got to the highway our scooters were unloaded and we were ready to head back to Darwin. I left wondering if I'd see Mick again, my friend confided that she rather fancied him and wondered if she'd made an impression. Two days later I had my answer, he found me. He was waiting for me outside the quarters when I came off shift at 6pm, we went to a drive-in movie that evening. Next morning, he took me to the jewellers and bought me a ring, a tiny diamond solitaire in a tiffany setting.

Our courtship was short but exciting, I was with Mick whenever possible on days off. We spent most of our time out on the plains. The manager of Jimmy Creek lent us his four-wheel drive so that we could get to the remote corners and more history of the area was revealed. Professional barramundi fishermen would use the station tracks to access Shady Camp, a resting place for buffalo hunters in earlier times, and net the tidal Mary River, then truck their catch back to Darwin. At Point Stuart Station, marked by palm trees were the lonely graves of four Japanese airmen shot down during WWII, I heard stories of adventures, rescue missions and misadventures. One property we visited had a crocodile skull on display which was easily two meters long. Sights like the magnificent water lilies and deep pink lotus floating on billabongs stayed with me, the amazing birdlife, pygmy geese in their hundreds and jabiru, ever so graceful. I was so fortunate to see it all before the tourist influx of today.

> There is a book written by Tom Cole, a former buffalo shooter and crocodile hunter about his years in the Northern Territory, and the people who formed its legends and shaped its spirit, which makes interesting reading.

Father had begun to work for WA State Shipping. He sailed between Fremantle, Barrow Island and Darwin, so next time he was in port it was time to introduce Mick to the family. He was naturally nervous at meeting my father, but after the introduction and a couple of beers, they both relaxed and the evening went okay, in father's words 'the sheep had been separated from the goats'. It was planned that Mick would write to mother introducing himself and stating his intentions, then when father got back to Fremantle he would vouch for

Mick and all would be well. Permission to proceed granted. Mother's reaction at the news that I wanted to marry Mick was, "Oh! my poor child, your life will be over".

My parents came to Darwin for the wedding, mother with a long face, nothing suited her, the accommodation my friend's parents provided in their own home not up to her standard. She was quite frankly being a bore, moaning and groaning. This wasn't about her; she wasn't in the limelight. When she saw the seating plan for the reception and noted that she would be sitting with our officiating priest she was furious, father would be partnering Mick's mother. With hindsight I guess she was sad, as her daughter was getting married her own marriage was falling apart.

I'd sent fabric to mother as she wanted to make my wedding dress and Barbara's gown. Our gowns didn't match the pictures or patterns I'd sent. She had made the dresses to her idea of what was acceptable and appropriate, skimping on the sleeves – Barbara's had little cape sleeves and my elbow length sleeves were almost straight, they were meant to be big full bells. She then complained that my bridesmaid's gown was more ornate than the one she'd made for me stating, "It would appear someone was trying to overshadow me". She was rude to our friends and acted like a spoiled brat but ultimately none of it mattered – it was my wedding not her big day.

I'd had my heart set on a two-tone dress, the bodice white and the skirt a shade of sapphire blue overlaid with heavy white guipure lace and wanted a bouquet of Arum lilies. The reaction to my wish was met with a stone wall, I was told in no uncertain terms that my selection was completely unacceptable, as a young bride I would be wearing all white and Arum lilies were funereal so most unsuitable. I compromised again and wore a white dress and carried a bouquet of 'Peace Roses'.

Father had to fly in from Barrow Island in order to be there and to walk me down the aisle, to give my hand to Mick. A quaint custom going back to when women were considered chattels, very traditional. Things were still rather conventional in 1966; Mick broke with convention electing for himself and his attendants not to wear jackets. It was after all the wet season again with high humidity and afternoon storms building.

My best friend Betty was chief bridesmaid and Barbara was my junior bridesmaid, Barbara had had an accident and broken her ankle and was wearing a plaster cast, the long gown hid it well and I was so proud and happy to have her there with me on my big day, she looked lovely and quite grown up. We got into hot water for taking her to the hotel for drinks with us after the wedding rehearsal, did mother really think so little of our judgement, we were responsible adults, we would take care of her.

The daughter of our Emcee was our flower girl. Mick's attendants were two of his mates, work colleagues. His father wasn't able to come to our wedding but his mother was there. The remainder of our guests were our new friends and colleagues. We were married on the 11th November 1966, Armistice Day, the anniversary of the signing of the peace treaty at the end of WWI, a significant date, one to remember. The actual wedding ceremony was almost like an out of body experience, well-rehearsed and ran like clockwork, we posed for photos, the local paper did a story on us, we made the social page. The reception, the toasts, the speeches, cutting the cake, tossing the bouquet and garter, what a day it was, certainly one I remember.

My parents had limited our guest list as they were paying for the meal at our reception. Our hosts had done themselves proud, the wedding banquet was superb, the centre piece a magnificent barramundi, ornately decorated, and an array of salads and side dishes. I don't remember eating anything, just floating on a cloud of happiness. Our cake was 2 tiered, decorated with candy roses. Mick was paying the bar tab so we asked our hosts not to clear the buffet after the formalities were over, having arranged an open bar for the friends that we wanted to share our day with, we'd sent out separate invitations, asking them to come for drinks after the formalities. We also had an instalment plan to pay for the drinks, it took us three months to clear the tab. We stayed at the same hotel where the reception was held, a chilled bottle of champagne was waiting for us in the bridal suite, we sat out on the balcony overlooking Fanny Bay and toasted our future.

- The Vietnam War was raging, the battle of Long Tan was fought on the day we announced our engagement. 18/08/1966.
- The federal election on the 5th of November 1966 was won by the Liberal National party coalition, Harold Holt was appointed our new Prime Minister. His name was destined to go down in the history books for other reasons.

Next morning Mick's mate picked us up and took us out to the airport to meet our plane. Our honeymoon was spent on Coburg Peninsula; Mick had been posted there as relief ranger; the buffalo sheds having shut down for the season. He had petitioned his boss to allow me to come as well instead of one of the other stock inspectors, disclaimers signed I was allowed to fly in with him. Coburg Peninsula is the northern most tip of the Northern Territory, originally the chosen location for the capital city of Port Essington, repeated cyclones altered those plans and the site was abandoned.

The peninsula was now a nature reserve and remote ranger station, observation post for coastal surveillance, reporting on insurgent boats and or aircraft sightings and frontline quarantine, fear of rabies and foot and mouth disease entering Australia. Across the bay was the pearl farm of Knocker Bay, just a boat ride away. So, for Mick it was a working honeymoon, for me it was another adventure. Coastal surveillance required twice daily reporting to headquarters in Canberra. We had a Landrover and a motor boat to use for patrols and other duties, a two-way radio for communication, we were supplied with a .303 rifle and .38 revolver. The typical Williams hut served as accommodation.

There was also a large shed to accommodate the boat and vehicle with an area set to one side as a workshop. The Ranger had a fenced vegetable garden which needed care and a "pet" python in a cage which needed feeding and looking after. It apparently liked to eat frogs. The best way to catch frogs is to leave the cover off the kettle, best frog trap ever. There were also many uncaged reptiles free ranging. We cooked on an open fire/BBQ mostly, although the hut did have a gas stove and there was a refrigerator.

The principal reason the AIB had selected Mick for this rotation, was his experience as a stockman. The Department Research Station near Darwin was working on trying to find a way to make cattle more resistant to the cattle tick. Ticks were causing considerable problems for the cattle industry; they caused an illness called 'Red Water', which led to heavy losses unless the cattle were resistant. The constant irritation of tick bites caused a condition known as 'ill thrift', weight loss etc. Additionally, bites and rubbing due to irritation marked the hides which were then not suitable for tanning into leather. The idea was to try cross breeding various breeds to see which cross would be most tick resistant, there was a herd of wild Balinese Bantang cattle running on Coburg Peninsular, left from the previous attempt of European settlement. The plan was to capture some of these breeding females and transport them to the Research Station for the crossbreeding programme.

There was an old cattle yard and a soak for watering near the airstrip and hut. First job was to cut bush rails and repair the yards making them secure enough to hold wild cattle. The second was to clean out the soak to get fresh water for the animals, once yarded. He had three weeks to achieve this. We worked together on these jobs, still had plenty of time for swimming, fishing and exploring. Took delivery of fuel and supplies from the coastal trader and spent a pleasant evening out on the boat as guests of the captain.

Then we had a visit from a team of Japanese men working on the pearl farm, asking for fresh meat. Only one of them spoke English,

I was led to believe they had visas to work at the pearl farm but not to go anywhere else, especially not to the nature reserve. Mick called the department on the two-way radio, it seemed they had an 'arrangement' with the permanent Ranger. On the way back to their boat they spotted an orchid high up in one of the trees, one of the men tried to climb up to get it but failed, Mick forbade them from cutting the tree to get the orchid. They left and we didn't see them again. They sent a photo taken during their visit to Mick, care of the Department in Darwin thanking us for our hospitality.

A couple of days before we were due to return to Darwin a team of stock inspectors were flown in to capture the cattle, safari style. It required men to leap from a moving vehicle, grab the beast by the tail and bring it down, then tie the legs with bull straps which they carried like bandoleers. In all, five adult cows, one bull and a female calf were captured. The animals were loaded onto a tilt trailer and transported to the yards where they were untied, then they were fed and had available water. A RAAF Dakota transport plane landed on our airstrip, the cattle were tranquillised and loaded into the plane for their flight to Darwin. When the last beast was being loaded, Mick stepped back, we all heard the crack when his ankle snapped. He was flown out with the cattle. One of the other stockmen stayed with me to pack up our gear and wait for the small aircraft that would take us back to Darwin later that afternoon. The permanent Ranger and his family were back, they came in on the same plane we were leaving on.

We'd had a lovely honeymoon, talked for hours, getting to really know each other, we exchanged stories of our early years and those of our parents, he told me about growing up in South Australia, and his life before he met me, the prejudice he'd faced and the good times too. His life experiences sounded so exotic, he had to explain a lot of the practices and terminology to me. We'd swum in the warm sea, walked along the beach, caught and cooked fish, eaten oysters straight from the reef, baked our own bread. Explored the peninsular, saw red deer, wild pigs, Timor ponies and Balinese Bantang cattle, some wallabies and one dingo. There sure are a lot of exotic species roaming about in our reserves. I had learnt a lot during our three weeks on Coburg, how to shoot a rifle and pistol, that worrying about tomorrow is futile, just to live and enjoy today, everything would work out and you could adapt as necessary, material things were just baggage, that you didn't really need very much to love and live well. Perhaps I should tell you a little more about the man I married.

Mick was born on the 12th October 1939 in Hendon-Middlesex, England. He was the second son of Leonardus Theodoor Bailey and Alberta Mary Bailey nee Steer. During WWII he and his brother Leonard John were evacuated to the country and stayed with a foster family in rural England to keep them safe. His father served in the RAF in the Middle East and his mother worked with the "WAVES", Women Approved Volunteer Emergency Service.

When the war ended, his parents like so many others, decided to leave England and move to Australia. What had attracted them was the Australian Government policy of 'populate or perish' and the active recruitment of British immigrants, offering assisted passage with a two-year bond. The State Government of South Australia had a planned industrial expansion programme, however, there was an acute housing shortage so the satellite cities of Elizabeth and Salisbury were planned to house the labour-force and their families needed for the industrialisation. The State Housing Trust was responsible for this project.

The family were initially housed at the Finsbury Immigration Hostel, then allocated a Trust home in Woodville North. Mick's father was employed as an architectural draftsman by the Trust, his civilian occupation prior to WWII, working on the satellite city project. He continued his studies; in 1959 he was registered as an architect in South Australia. In 1964 he was elected an Associate of the Royal Australian Institute of Architects. Mick's mother worked at the 'Pope' factory, a manufacturer of electrical goods, on the assembly line, later she studied nursing and after graduation worked with disabled children for many years in a specialised hospital. Mick's father had grown up in the Netherlands and spoke English with a Dutch accent, Mick and John attended Christian Brothers College. These two details resulted in the family being viewed with suspicion in the neighbourhood. Woodville North was a 'blue collar' area, class distinction was the norm in Australia at the time. English immigrants were considered a 'threat' and private schools snobbish. The majority of the children attending the State schools, so life was often turbulent for the Bailey boys, it took some time to stake their claim in the neighbourhood. Ultimately the family was accepted and new friendships formed.

The Woodville area had once been rural and there were still pockets where there were stables, horses were still being used by some vendors for deliveries. Mick said he was drawn to this part of the neighbourhood and developed friendships with some of the stable owners, he was soon out riding in the paddocks after school. His parents sent the boys on a holiday camp down on the Eyre Peninsular one summer which he loved and cemented his longing for living on the land. He was good at sports and represented South Australia at the junior swimming championships and played lacrosse for the State Team. He attended Urrbrae Agricultural High School for two years, spending time on a wheat farm during the summer break. Toward the end of the second year the students were shown the film "Back of Beyond", a documentary about the Birdsville mailman, Tom Cruze. Mick asked the projectionist how a person could get to live and work out in that part of Australia. He was told that he would need to go and contact a stock and station agent and ask about employment.

As soon as school finished that year Mick went into the city office of 'Elders GM' to inquire about working in the outback. It must have been one of those 'fateful days' the owner of a cattle station was in Adelaide and looking for young workers. Mick met with him and within a couple of days was on his way to Granite Downs Station in the north of South Australia. He soon learnt that the life wasn't a glamorous one, that it meant long days in the saddle, extremes of temperature and harsh living conditions, with a poor diet of damper and salt beef being the usual fare. He started his 'apprenticeship' with the camp cook, the head-stockman taking an interest in him and teaching him 'the ropes'.

At the end of the muster the cattle were walked to the railhead to be sent to market. As a test of his abilities, he was given the job of taking the horses back to the station, following the same route back. He arrived back at the station with 2 more horses than he started with and was deemed to have proven his worth as a stockman. He worked on Tieyon and New Crown Stations, employed as 'horse-tailer', in charge of looking after the horses, bringing in the horse-plant for the days muster and watching the horses during the day to ensure they were on good feed. At night there were a number of horses kept near the stock-camp for the night-watch, and the horses for the next day's work were hobbled so that they would be easier to bring in the following morning. In addition to being hobbled a couple wore a bell around their neck making it easier to locate them in the pre-dawn. Each of the stockmen had a number of horses to rotate so that they remained fresh and not overworked.

Mick's life was rarely without incident. He attended a muster of adjoining properties, each property would send a stock-camp to sort out any unbranded cattle from the boundary areas, as there weren't any fences and the cattle 'free-ranged'. Cows and calves were 'mothered' and any unbranded stock divided between neighbours and branded with the station brands. In the early morning just before daylight while bringing in the horses, Mick broke his ankle, riding boots not the best choice for running over rough ground in the half-light.

On another occasion he was sent out to a bore to man the 'pump-jack', a diesel driven pump to bring water up when there was no wind for the windmill. He was left alone with some supplies to refuel the motor and keep the belt drive operating. During the belt maintenance his hand got caught in the cogs, severely lacerating his finger. He said that he plunged his hand into a bag of flour to staunch the bleeding and proceeded to walk to the homestead, knowing it would be at least a week before anyone came out to check on him, carrying his bridle, he was hoping to catch a horse along the way. A severe thunder storm broke while he was out on the plain, making the journey more treacherous, he walked all night arriving at the station well after sun-up. They sent him to Alice Springs Hospital for treatment.

Mick told me many more stories about desert adventures and characters he met in places like Oodnadatta, Maree, where he purchased his prized "Scobie" stock whip and The Finke, all places along the 'Ghan Railway' which follows the trail of the early explorers and camel drivers.

A mob of cattle, destined for Lake Torrens Station in South Australia were sent by rail to Hawker, Mick volunteered to accompany them on the journey and walk them from the railhead out to the station. The manager not being experienced with cattle, offered Mick a job so he stayed on. Lake Torrens had previously been solely a sheep station. A deep friendship developed with this family, they treated Mick like a family member, not just as an employee. Lake Torrens was within a day's travel from Adelaide and Mick's mother was often a guest. Meanwhile his father had moved to Melbourne after the South Australian Housing Trust project was completed. Mick's grandmother had come to live with them after retiring and leaving the family farm in Cornwall, her youngest son John taking over. Mick's mother, who hated her name Alberta, now called herself 'Audrey', two of his uncles had left the UK and settled in New Zealand.

Mick bought a motor bike and would ride to Adelaide to visit his family, he also bought a small yacht and surf board, enjoying holidays on the water. When one of the station dogs - a border collie had pups, he chose one for his mother, she loved the dog and named him Mr. Bigalow, which was the cause of much amusement when she was introduced to a human Mr. Bigalow. In 1960 Mick went on a holiday to visit his uncles in New Zealand. On his return he decided that in order to follow his career and ultimately become a Station Manager he needed wider experience, so he set off for Queensland.

In Queensland he worked on numerous properties in different parts of the State, among them, the channel country around Thargomindah and Eromanga, the Brigalow around Springsure, and in the Diamantina and Georgina River areas. Different styles of mustering and management were used in each of these regions. On a property in the Diamantina, he was employed as Overseer. The Overseer was the link between the owner and the general staff, reporting on aspects of the general progress of stockwork, the expectation being that he was to dine with the family whenever the stock-camp was at the station. Not something that Mick liked very much, after a day's work he just wanted to have a meal and settle for the night, not socialise and have an elaborate dinner late in the evening. He told of having committed a 'faux-pas' one evening by making a long drink out of the owners 'special rum', which was to be savoured and highly praised. His action was severely frowned upon.

It was also on this property that 'the worst experience ever' (his words) befell him. The best horses were kept at the station in the house horse-paddock, they were trucked out to the yards for the drafting and branding of the calves as needed then returned to be spelled and given special rations. Everything was made ready and the horses loaded; the Bronco mare a part Percheron heavy horse, affectionately called 'Mummy' and the Camp horse 'Wernadinga', the Camp horse is the one trained to shoulder beasts out of the mob so they can be roped and worked on, the one reserved for the Overseer or Head Stockman, Mick's mount. They set off along the track and disaster struck, the floor boards of the truck had rotted over time, and because they were covered with sand to give the horses traction during transportation no one had noticed this, they had given way and the horses fallen through. They were both so badly injured there was nothing that could be done to save them. He said no-one blamed him for the accident, but he never forgave himself, saying it was his responsibility to ensure that everything was done right. He left the property shortly afterwards and headed further west to the land of the Min-Min light around Boulia.

It was from there that a group of ringers, (stockmen) decided to head to Mt Isa for the Rodeo. The horse named 'Spinifex' was the main attraction. It was also one of the first times that the event was held under lights. Mick's ride was late in the day, his horse spooked by the shadows fell and rolled, Mick was badly injured, his mates helped him back out to the station but he was unable to stand erect let alone work, so had no option but to go back to Mt Isa for medical treatment. Luck was with him, although he had two ruptured disks in his lumber spine, a surgeon recently returned from training in the UK operated on him and performed a spinal fusion. The nerves in his back were so badly bruised it took a full year of intensive physiotherapy, with nerve blocks, before he was able to be discharged.

He returned to Adelaide and began the journey back to full health. Initially he couldn't do very much and concentrated on walking and swimming to build up his muscles, then needing an income he purchased a lunch bar in the city, he retained the staff who worked the shop front, taking care of ordering and deliveries, stacking shelves and that type of work himself. He had a loyal customer base and the business did well enough, he sold the business before the lease was due to end. As he got stronger, he bought a horse and trained it as a polocrosse pony. Within a year he was back riding and playing polocrosse and working at the Gepps Cross sale-yards. He said he didn't feel settled and was yearning to go back to the life he'd known before the accident. His father sent him an advertisement from the Northern Territory Gazette, the administration was recruiting Stock Inspectors. He applied, was interviewed and chosen for a position in Darwin. He sold the horse, bought a Holden Ute and headed north, taking his working dog to Lake Torrens and leaving her with his friends. Then driving to Darwin to take up his position in 1965.

On returning to Darwin after our honeymoon, our first hurdle was to get Mick mended; his injury meant he was on sick leave so our honeymoon was extended. We had secured a caretaker tenancy in the home of one of his colleagues who was south on annual leave. This was a godsend as housing was at a premium in Darwin, also there was a very strict criteria to meet for married quarters, let alone a house. We had tried the State Housing Authority but didn't qualify. As we had met and married in Darwin it was assumed that we would have had a roof over our heads, single men's hostel and nursing quarters weren't actually suitable anymore but! …. Again, we didn't qualify for short term married quarters either, so caretaker tenancies were our best option. We had three weeks to get over this hurdle.

Ultimately after much searching and many rejections, Mick went to his boss for advice. Miraculously a room in the married quarters became available just as our landlords returned at the end of their holiday. Phew, no questions asked, just a bottle of the best rum left on someone's office desk. Mick's poor dog, his bullterrier Candy, had to spend much of the time in the back of his Ute, under the tarpaulin sheltering from the rain or in the cabin. At night we smuggled her into our room, it was one of those places where the walls didn't quite reach the ceiling or the floor, our single beds were of different heights as well, so much for married quarters. Meals in the dining room were not actually Michelin Star but were included in the rent so we ate them, ordered a picnic lunch most days so we could get out of the place.

After his recovery from the broken ankle Mick was put on quarantine duties at the harbour, most days he was in the office but then a ship arrived requiring quarantine inspection, Mick hadn't been vaccinated against a range of tropical diseases so he was rushed through and immunised for the lot on a single visit, needless to say his reaction to so many was extreme. His fever was dangerously high, I draped him with wet towels under the fan to try to cool him, he was so bad that he was delirious. I was frightened, forced him to take fluids and aspirin, gradually he got better and came through. The ship in the meantime had been and sailed off into the wide blue yonder. We managed to get another caretaker tenancy.

Mick was now at the Darwin Abattoir doing meat inspection, we had moved into our new temporary home. These people had many caged birds to be taken care of, the under-croft of the house was a partitioned giant birdcage, only the section with the laundry was clear. In addition, there were aviaries in the gardens full of exotic parrots. They had also left us a dog to care for, a poor bedraggled, skinny, mangy, miserable border collie. She was named Lady, Mick's Candy and Lady became friends, our mission was to get Lady well, daily swims in the sea to cure the mange, a thorough worming and flea control, gentle exercise to get her fit again. Feeding was another matter, she was so starved that she could only manage a tiny amount, then only if she was hand fed. Gradually she got better, her coat grew back, her eyes brightened and she had more energy, she put on weight and was so much happier. Our tenancy was drawing to a close. I wasn't prepared to leave Lady behind when we moved on. Mick didn't ask, he told them we were keeping the dog, they seemed pleased.

The birds were another story, gradually the quails disappeared, we couldn't find any holes where they could have got out, the predator came from above, a python was getting in and having a feast. Then the side fell out of one of the big parrot cages, the birds were free, the wire holding it together had rusted through. The birds lived in the trees now but only for a few days, then they didn't bother to come back for their daily seed ration.

When the dry season began, I travelled around the top-end stations with Mick as he was undertaking his duties, vaccinating horses against 'Strangles', treating others with 'swamp cancer', my nursing skills useful as his veterinary assistant. The smaller holdings in the top-end were also trialling pasture improvement and more intensive operations in livestock management. Interesting times and fascinating countryside and people from so many different walks of life.

We received some wonderful wedding gifts, some ultra practical like dinner sets, a canteen of cutlery, bed linen and bath towels, a set of cookware. Others beautiful to look at, like the blue glass bowl I still have and demi-tasse coffee sets, wine glasses and water sets. The one we used and prized most in that first year was a 6-cup thermos, we took that with us whenever we were on the road. The most sentimental was given to us by the young German couple from Jimmy's Creek. We'd come home from a night out to find them sitting in their open top four-wheel drive vehicle a tarpaulin draped over them and the baby to keep the rain off. They'd come to Darwin for supplies to tide them over the wet season and brought us a gift. A pair of hollow stem champagne glasses, to this day I feel they must have come from a set they had been given at their wedding, they'd had so little themselves when we stayed with them at Jimmy's Creek. I have treasured them since and still have them.

We had more big news, we were going to be parents. Exciting but terrifying at the same time. Our house-sit was almost over, we now had two dogs, four tea-chests of wedding presents, four suitcases, the swag and tucker box. Mick's Holden Ute, his government issue Falcon Ute and a baby on the way. I had sold my scooter to one of the other girls at the hospital. Mick was posted to Elliot, a very timely transfer out of Darwin to a small town half way between Darwin and Alice Springs.

Mother's reaction to the news of the arrival of our firstborn was unexpected, she cried and said that she was 'far too young to be a grandmother.' I was 20 she 47. It wasn't quite what I'd expected to hear, then she composed herself and tried to be happy for us. Her earlier prediction that my life was over couldn't have been more wrong. It was about to really start.

***

I'm All Grown Up Now

Childhood and school days are meant to prepare us for our journey into the world, but in my case, I was about to experience a world I knew very little about. The Australian outback, it's people, isolation, industries, customs, taboos, it's hospitality, diversity, challenges, hardships, camaraderie, resilience, but most of all it's utter beauty and changeability. A timeless place where you could lose yourself or find your true self.

The world around us was seeing more change, man was about to walk on the Moon, the war in Vietnam was finally drawing to a close and our troops were coming home. Unfortunately, not to the hero's welcome they deserved; it wasn't 'a popular war'. Our young men and women puppets in a political chess game that was unwinnable, the tide of turn too strong, the aftermath as tragic as the war itself. Civil wars that tear a nation apart history has shown, end with no winners, just many broken lives. The repercussions of our involvement were about to unfold globally and here at home.

Out in the inland life went on fairly much as if none of this was happening, it revolved around the here and now of daily living. Country music shows travelled from town to town. Hawkers still travelled from place to place with everything a household needed in the back of their vehicles, from pots and pans to clothing and everything imaginable in-between. The mail still the most eagerly awaited event. So much more came on the mail truck, not just letters, it was a lifeline as important as the Flying Doctor Service.

Picnic race meetings were held, usually at the end of 'The Muster', the culmination of a year's work. The stations bringing their best horses. The long weekend extended by a few more days to host a gymkhana with events like calf roping, barrel racing and tent pegging. Rodeo, young men showing off their talents on horseback, bull riding, the festivities ending with a Rodeo Ball, a reason to get dressed up in your finest attire, for young people to meet and celebrate life. People gathered from far and wide within the district and formed quite a large camp, reminiscent of a small town that was packed up and gone the morning after the Ball. Station trucks loaded up, towing horse floats, Utes packed high with swags and camping gear, convoys heading back to the start of another year's work. Quite a few sore heads and bleary eyes, but a great time was had by all.

The flying Padre visited isolated cattle stations in his canvas covered tiger moth and showed his movies in exchange for av-gas and hospitality. His sermons listened to by all from owners, managers to stockmen and their families, the community that enabled a cattle station to function. If we were in the area we were invited to stay. The flying doctor base was the main lifeline for communication as well as healthcare. We had two-way radios for long and short distance communication and a party-line telephone, which was not always reliable so we still mainly used telegrams for urgent communication. The 'Mail' so eagerly awaited, so much came by mail - letters and parcels, catalogues to order from, library books, newspapers and even our grocery order. Living at Elliott was a coming of age for me. I realised how ill prepared for my new life I really was and had much to learn.

A brief description of the township of Elliott, it is halfway between Darwin and Alice Springs on the Stuart Highway. It had been a strategic point during WWII, had a long airstrip, with a shed terminus building, so it was ideal for the Flying Doctor Service. Monthly clinics were held at the Police Station, which had a clinic adjacent to it. The people from surrounding stations and small roadhouse communities came to attend the doctor. Flying Doctor days were also a social event and good trade for the local hotel, café and general store.

The policeman posted here was married to a nursing sister who ran the clinic for day-to-day problems. She could communicate directly with the doctors based in Alice Springs if needed, so effectively she was a nurse practitioner. The nearest hospitals were at Tennant Creek and Katherine, both considerable distances away. If a road ambulance was needed it usually came from Tennant Creek.

The little town was also the base for other important services and infrastructure, there were depots for Roads and Telecommunications, a single teacher primary school, also a fuel and truck depot, general store, hotel and café which included the telephone exchange and post office agency. Public servants based there were the Police officer, Nursing sister, Road Works Manager, a telecom technician, an Aboriginal Welfare officer, the AIB Stock Inspector, a teacher and an environmental officer. His task was to trial various tree species to see which would establish around the various watering points along the stock routes. The reason that most trees did not survive was that fact that during the dry seasons the black soil of the plain dried out and deep cracks formed, breaking the tree roots which consequently caused them to fail.

Elliott faced the Stuart Highway on the western side, a side street to the north was where the high-set Government houses stood, these had the accommodation upstairs, with official offices and parking underneath. Two other streets ran parallel to the highway where the older homes stood alongside three new ones. A village for Aboriginal families was located in the last street, hence the need for the school. Local employment was on surrounding cattle stations or within the township itself, supporting the various government departments and businesses.

Our house was on the south side of town about a kilometre out, set back from the highway to allow for road train parking out front. The yard was fenced, the block approximately 2000^{sq} metres. On the road setback planted at intervals were Sturt's Desert Rose shrubs, the floral emblem of the Northern Territory, surrounded by a circle of Sturt's desert pea groundcovers, the floral emblem of South Australia. Tourists frequently stopped to take photographs of these when in full bloom. They looked so amazing against the bare red earth.

The house was high-set, L-shaped, kitchen was in the foot of the L, the living and bedrooms in the vertical. The rooms were separated from the outside walls by louvred corridors forming a breezeway on either side. There were 2 main bedrooms, a lounge-dining room. At the kitchen end of the corridor was a storage cupboard, at the other end the bathroom. The northern corridor was divided into 2 sleepouts and an entry, with landing and stairs outside. Most people used the stairs to the verandah and kitchen. The under-croft was used for parking. The office was under the N-E corner of the house and the laundry under the kitchen. There was an established garden with patches of lawn divided by earth pathways.

A magnificent poinciana tree shaded the house to the east and there was a row of athel pines along the front fence. Bauhinia trees were dotted down the southern side. Additionally, there was a chicken run and a fenced vegetable plot. A BBQ area sat outside the infrequently used "front steps", edged by sweet smelling oleander shrubs. In addition to a gas stove, there was a slow combustion wood stove in the kitchen and a slow combustion heater in the living room. It gets cold during the 'dry' in the inland. The house was fully furnished.

Although our arrival was expected, there were still handovers to be done, and the people who were transferring out weren't quite ready. They had recently had a new addition to the family and with 2 small children and a baby, the poor woman had her hands full. The men headed off so that Mick could meet the station people and get familiar with procedures and processes. Meanwhile I was introduced to the township and its women. It didn't take them long to see how 'green' I was and lots of advice followed. I was welcomed and invited to the CWA lifestyle. Back at the house I was warned to be very vigilant if Mick was late, especially if he'd been to the pub ... apparently it was very easy for men to get disorientated when coming home in a state of inebriation, this causing confusion, particularly with respect to the location of the bathroom. Previous male occupants of the house had been known to confuse the storage cupboard for the bathroom.

I tried not to laugh, didn't quite believe what I was hearing, until I overheard the man of the house telling Mick the same thing. Dinner that night was steak and bread with tomato sauce. The meal itself wasn't unusual fare in the outback but the cooking method certainly took me aback. The fire was stoked, the stove-top was almost glowing, then the steak was dropped directly onto the stove, it sizzled and smoked was turned and did the same, then it was plonked onto plates and handed around. Not a pan in sight, who needs a BBQ, this was the indoor version. I must have looked shocked, was assured it was ok and that the heat was sufficient to keep the stove-top clean enough. I'd grown up with mother's wood stove in Toodyay and Northcliffe which was regularly scrubbed and polished with stove black. My experience in the kitchen was limited, but this didn't seem quite right. Neither did swishing a bucket of soapy water down the length of the room, then sweeping it out the door seem the right way to wash the floor, but I was told it was ok too, it would dry quickly enough.

Mick's position at Elliot was one of considerable responsibility in furthering the developments of the cattle industry in the Northern Territory, both in the economic sense and with regard to animal health and welfare. He was involved in disease eradication programmes to control TB and Brucellosis through testing and vaccination, and maintaining a permit system to track travelling livestock. This was in place to enable trace-back in the event of outbreaks of disease, foot and mouth disease was greatly feared. Elliot was the Tick Line, the control point to prevent outbreaks of "Red Water" sickness.

Handover completed we took up residence, the Falcon Ute went back to Darwin, our government issue vehicle was a Toyota Land cruiser. I assisted Mick in any way I could with administration and accompanied him whenever possible to meet the station people and learn more about outback life. My bread baking improved, shown how by the wife of a station manager and through watching and talking to camp cooks who used camp-ovens sunk into a hole in the ground, half filled with coals then the oven placed on top of them, covered with more coals and soil placed over the top to keep the heat in. An empty jam tin placed in the centre of the oven separating four balls of dough ensured even heat distribution and made for a perfect golden crust. An amazing way to bake bread, delicious roasts and stews made the same way. One that Mick was very familiar with as he'd used this method from a young age when cooking in the stock-camps and stations around Alice Springs, in the north of South Australia and over in Queensland. Damper being his preferred loaf. Damper had another advantage, it only required self-raising flour, and was quick to make and bake. Whereas bread needed yeast and proving time, not ideal when on the move. Cakes were not my forte; I almost choked Candy, Mick's bull terrier when she tried to eat my failed sponge cake and it got stuck in her gullet. Gradually I learnt more tricks and ideas for using salted beef and our menu options grew.

Our baby boy was born on the 27th September 1967 at Katherine Hospital. Cause for much rejoicing and celebration. I had everything ready for him, had spent hours sewing just like mother had before my sister was born. I'd made a quilt for his cot out of the satin remnants of my wedding dress, he never needed it, I think we only used it for his christening photos. The end of September is hot in the Northern Territory, he didn't need the shawl or layette mother had sent, complete with beanie and booties. It was a beautiful piece of handiwork. Grandmother (*Oma*) had also sent parcels from Germany with beautiful baby clothes and the best gift of all, muslin nappies to go with his little singlets.

Mick arranged a big party, people came from far afield to help wet this baby's head, local ladies came loaded with food to help cater. The party went till daylight, then the BBQ was lit, everyone had steak and eggs for breakfast served with the huge basket of bread rolls I'd baked. We named him Brenton Michael Bailey. 'Brenton' a name Mick liked; he'd had a mate as a boy named co-incidentally 'Brenton Bailey'. Michael for his father, although Mick had always been Mick right from a little boy.

When living in towns and cities there is a support service for new mothers at the Infant Health Clinic, in the bush it's a bit different.

A friend from one of the stations lent me a set of baby scales to monitor and record progress. I was enrolled with the baby clinic in Camooweal, a town across the border in Queensland, this service was attached to the Flying Doctor Service. They sent a book to record the baby's progress and through correspondence and leaflets they taught young mothers about introducing solid foods, baby food recipes, and general advice about baby care, from colic, cradle cap, and teething issues to nappy rash. Grandmother had sent me a set of small saucepans, 'cooking for one' size.

One evening when Mick came in from work, ravenous having missed lunch and driven a considerable distance, all that was prepared was a tiny meal for Brenton. It must have smelled good, the look of disappointment on his face was one not to forget, he asked what he could have. I offered to make eggs. He asked what I'd been doing all day, I told him I'd been watching the baby sleep. He went down to the pub that night for dinner and came home quite late!

We had chickens and ducks, a vegetable garden and pigs which were fed on scraps collected from the hotel and cafe. Most of our supplies came by road from Alice Springs, purchased in bulk, drums of flour and bags of sugar, cartons of tinned foods including milk powder. Local shopping was very expensive so only done in an emergency. There was a fairly constant stream of visitors from surrounding stations, and trucks stopping to have cattle inspected, or to collect movement permits, sometimes at odd hours during the night. Our menagerie grew, a drover retired and purchased the local café, his wife's favourite horse came to live with us. I learnt to ride on "Princess". We had added poddy calves, calves left behind by drovers, born on the trail, unable to keep up with the herd. I was given a little goat, I named him "Captain Silver".

Elliott is where the Murranji Stock Route ends at number 7 bore and becomes the Barkly Stock Route. So is strategically placed for cattle movements north and south along the Stuart Highway and west to east from Western Australia into Queensland. Number 7 bore was the tick-line quarantine station. I've mentioned before the issues of cattle tick in the top end country. If tick carrying cattle mixed with 'clean' cattle there was every chance that tick transferred to cattle who had not come in contact with this disease, and had no resistance. The parasite carried by the tick would cause "red-water" disease in the clean herd leading to huge economic loss and very sick cattle. Similar to the transmission of malaria in humans and paralysis tick in our domestic pets.

Stock routes were established by the Government to facilitate movement of cattle from remote parts of Australia to markets. Cattle would be mustered on the stations, saleable beasts put together into mobs and walked to the point of sale or railhead. Sometimes neighbours would combine herds. The beasts branded and earmarked to establish ownership, so droving or walking costs could be shared, at the point of sale the herd would be drafted again into mobs using this identification. The drover and his team would take control of these mobs and lead them to their destination. Animals can only walk a certain distance in a day and need time to feed along the way, hence the need for stock routes with watering points. Underground water was pumped up into earth tanks known as 'turkey nests' and means of getting the water up was via a bore-hole tapping into the underground reservoir, either using wind power or a diesel operated apparatus known as a pump jack. Sometimes the distance between watering points was greater than that which cattle could cover in a day.

These night camps were known as a dry stage, the riskiest stage as thirsty animals were likely not to settle and could be prone to 'rush' or stampede. Danger to man and beast alike. Night camps involved a watch, where the stockmen took turns to ride around the mob in two-hourly rotation to keep the cattle calm. Generally, there weren't any paddocks to put the cattle into overnight and the horses where generally hobbled out so they could feed, but not go too far. Sometimes several drovers would be travelling along the same stock route during a given season, so it was imperative that the mobs kept moving not only to meet deadlines at the other end of the journey, but to ensure there was sufficient feed for following mobs. Paddocks could be eaten out rather quickly leading to issues for others following along.

Changing times in the outback were ahead, progress can't be stopped. Drovers were slowly becoming redundant, road trains taking over the movement of cattle from station to railhead or markets. Disease control in livestock was making advances, we were at Elliott to witness the beginning of major change, but I was fortunate enough to see both sides, the pioneering ways and modern innovations. To meet the people who had done it the traditional way and those who risked a lot to embrace change.

I was there at a time early enough to witness the romance of the old ways in action, a time that poets had written about and country music artists sang about. I was having a wonderful life experience. I loved the open plain with the mirage on the horizon, the dusty winds called 'devil-devils', the majestic soaring eagles in bright blue cloudless skies, storms building and sudden downpours, the plain glistening in early morning sunshine after a rainstorm and the flush of new grass that followed. I loved the smell of horses. Most of all I loved the wonderful man who had made it possible.

I'd turned 21, officially an adult now, I was eligible to vote, I didn't feel any different on this my 'big day'. Mother sent me an embroidered table cloth as a gift with matching serviettes. Mick's mother sent a watch with a marcasite band that Mick had asked her to get for me. Mick also arranged for a surprise evening, he'd booked a babysitter, asked a friend to make a special cake and reserved dinner at the local hotel, to be served in the dining room not in the bar. He had to go down earlier in the day to meet trucks, was asked to come and have a beer. He declined, he told me later, telling them that there was a twenty-first birthday in the family, but they were persuasive, one beer wouldn't hurt. The Truckie announced the news, assuming that it was Mick's birthday and the bar turned on a party with beers flowing and games of pool and darts played. Oblivious to any of this I prepared a meal in my trusty pressure cooker and set the table with the new table cloth.

Mick came home a little worse for wear, picked up the pot and carried it to the table putting it down before I could put a mat under it. You can imagine what happened to the new table cloth, not only was the pot hot, it was sooty from the stove-top. Copious tears flowed, Mick explained what had happened, the babysitter came and went to tell the hotel people the sorry tale. We had dinner and cake the following day. The tablecloth was ruined but we never told mother.

One night Mick came home late, I was already asleep when he came in, so was only half awake when he told me he'd put the donkey in the chook house. Next morning, I woke to the most incredible noise, I'd never heard a donkey bray before. Mick had rescued the little one, a rather sad tale. The poor little guy, just a foal, had been run out of a mob of wild donkeys and he was being put up at a roadhouse as the prize in an auction to raise funds for the Flying Doctor. Mick had stopped in at the roadhouse on his way back from one of the stations where cattle had been dipped and he was needed to inspect the cattle and issue the permit to move stock if they were clear of ticks. Mick loved animals, especially dogs, horses and donkeys, he was outraged that these people could treat the little donkey in such a heartless manner. On his way out he put the donkey into the cabin of the Toyota and brought him back to Elliot. We had calf milk left from our poddy calves, so made up a bottle and gave the little one a feed. He grew into a lovely pet, very attached to Mick, if there was a pair of his jeans on the line the donkey would stand by them until Mick got home, then trot to meet him as he alighted from his vehicle.

Brenton often rode on 'Jack's' back, being led around the garden. Little donkeys grow into big ones, Mick found a good home for him with a famous travelling buckjump show, the owner's daughter had recently lost her jenny donkey. He was heading back to his property in Queensland and assured us the little one would have a safe good home for life, it was sad to see him go, he went willingly up the ramp into the horse truck, such a trusting little animal. Same story with the poddy calves, they grew big and strong and found homes on a cattle station nearby. The pigs became ham and bacon. Utes are ok for two people, not so useful as family cars, so Mick traded his for a sedan. The goat disgraced himself, he ruined the paintwork on our brand-new family car, Mick was unforgiving, Captain Silver had to go.

We had three interstate holidays during our time in Elliott, two to South Australia where I got to meet Mick's family, his father, grandmother, brother and his wife and their daughters. Brenton was baptised in Adelaide. The second time we went he was old enough to play with his cousins for the first time, three little girls. Our visit to WA coincided with father's visit home. Mick met the rest of my family, aunt Astrid and uncle Herbert, cousins Ilona and her husband Bob and little daughter Jodie, also Marianne who had just given birth to her first child, a little girl and cousin Ronald.

My 'little' sister was taller than me now, she was in high school, it was lovely to see her again, I had missed her very much. Mother didn't seem to know what to do with us, treated us like strangers that she was unsure about. Quite convinced that Mick came from an alien planet so she tiptoed around him as if walking on eggshells, he'd mentioned once that he sometimes liked a cold boiled potato (seasoned with salt and pepper) alongside his meat and salad, so she saved a bowl of leftover chips for him, next day making quite a show of presenting them to him in the back garden where he was sitting with Brenton. She did redeem herself later by making a pot of Hungarian goulash with dumplings, stew and dumplings being a favourite of Mick's.

We asked her to babysit one evening so that we could go out for a meal. I had a bad feeling and we left the restaurant early, when we got back, I could hear the baby crying, mother had him propped up on a pillow trying to feed him with a bottle, I couldn't understand why she was so reluctant to hold him in her arms, after all that is the natural way to hold a baby, particularly whilst feeding. Mick had hired a really nice car for our stay, father made disparaging comments about our choice of make and model, Mick suggested that he could get out and walk if he didn't like the transport. We left for the Territory early cutting short our stay.

Brenton took a tumble when he was learning to walk and broke a tooth, which got infected necessitating a trip to the hospital in Alice Springs. I got a ride down with a neighbouring station owner who was going down to Alice Springs to inspect another property, one he was in the process of purchasing, as Mick was really busy dipping cattle at Number 7. Mobs were being trucked and he had a drover with a walking mob in the holding paddock, another drover coming down the Murranji Stock Route, so he couldn't get time off. It was arranged I would get a ride back on one of the trucks coming from Alice Springs for the next load. When Brenton's tooth had been attended to, I was to go to the family of the station manager who was trucking cattle to Alice Springs, descendants of an Afghan family who had been camel drivers in the early days of the Territory. They had now diversified and trucks were the new camels. I was made very welcome and their hospitality was truly warm. After a meal of curry, the hottest I'd ever eaten, we set off in the truck, an International Semi, towing two trailers. Brenton settled in his makeshift bed on the floor of the passenger side, heading back north.

About an hour out of Alice Springs I noticed that the driver was nodding off into micro sleeps, the poor man had deadlines to keep, he told me this was his second night without sleep, but my little boy was at risk if we had an accident. To panic wasn't an option, bravado took over and resilience to the fore, I insisted on taking over, I was shown the controls and how to gauge the engine performance using the rev counter. I drove into the night, baby asleep on the floor of the truck, the driver asleep in the passenger seat. Fortunately, we didn't encounter any horses or cattle on the road, I didn't slow for any of the little towns or hamlets along the way, just concentrated on keeping the truck on the road ahead at an even speed. By the time daylight came my eyes were burning but our driver had woken up and the baby was about to. We pulled into the Renner Springs roadhouse which wasn't that far from Elliott. Time for Brenton and myself to alight from the vehicle so that the truck could continue on to collect the next load. The roadhouse proprietor managed to get Mick on the two-way. The last load was about to leave the dip, so Mick could get away to come and get us. Everyone was relieved, all the deadlines were met, the cattle trucks made it to the railhead, the drover went east with his mob and the next one still had 2 days to reach Elliott. Brenton was on the mend, Mick and I were exhausted, strangely my legs had turned to jelly once the adrenaline of the night wore off. We were all safe and together again.

Thankfully *"There were **NO** lights coming over the hill to blind me."* Borrowed with apology, a line from a song by Slim Dusty.

Our dogs had puppies within a day of each other, Lady had 4, Candy had trouble, only one of her pups survived and sadly she didn't make it either. We had an orphaned pup, Lady had to foster the little one. She regularly took it away and buried it like an old bone, eventually after several days she gave up and accepted her fate. We also had two cats, a ginger tom and a calico female. Mick's mother came to visit bringing her border collie with her. Mick was very happy to be able to show his mother where we were living and how his working life played out. She stayed for about ten days during which time Mick took her out around his station run, which she enjoyed. I was glad when she left. She told us about a young woman who had left a blue heeler named' Sue' behind when she lost her fight with cancer. This dog was looking to be rehomed and she asked if Mick would take her, naturally he said yes. Sue duly arrived, she was a beautiful dog and fitted into our menagerie perfectly.

There was a lot of rain that summer and the creeks and inland lakes flooded, grass was plentiful everywhere and as is not uncommon in Australia, plagues follow a good season. First it was the locusts, then the marsupial rats, they were everywhere in huge numbers, nothing was safe from them. They chewed the wiring in the cars, ate through garden hoses and did much more damage. The dogs and cats got tired of hunting them; Lady was particularly good at catching them but she eventually gave up too. Everyone had drum traps set up and a competition of who could catch the most in a night began. We needed the Pied Piper, then just as suddenly it stopped. The rodents seemed to disappear overnight.

Father had given us a radio, it was ancient, a shortwave valve radio, I think it may have been one he had rebuilt. I recall him giving Mick a list of instructions and some spare parts. As I've previously said communication wasn't the best back then and that included radio reception. Shortwave bands would sometimes find a program you could listen to, but generally all you got were bubbles and crackles. Some station friends came to the house on Melbourne Cup Day hoping to listen to the race. We prepared lunch and settled back to listen to the broadcast, for once we had nice clear reception. In the final stages of the race the radio died, nothing, Mick tried everything father had told him but to no avail, the wonderful radio was dead. We didn't find out that 'Rain Lover' won the Cup that year for a long time. Our friends left laughing and in good humour. Mick took the back off and all the valves had turned black, burnt out, the radio really was dead.

We were concerned that the utopian bubble of the fully furnished house supplied by the Administration could one day be snatched away. Being without a backup plan now that we had a family wasn't such a good idea. Mick bought a caravan, our assurance of a roof over our heads and best of all, it was mobile and could come wherever life took us.

When Brenton was two years old, we found out our family was about to grow, a baby was going to join us in the middle of the following year. That wasn't to be the only change to our lives.

4

A Change of Direction

Mick's goal from the time he'd left home to become a stockman had been to one day manage a cattle station, to be able to put his knowledge and the experience he'd acquired working on a wide range of properties, in many different parts of the Northern Territory, top end of South Australia and in Queensland together and do the 'top job'. A graduation in a way, to demonstrate his abilities. The owner of the two station properties that surrounded the town of Elliott had recently purchased a third property near Alice Springs, one of his managers was relocating to the new place leaving a vacancy. Mick was on good terms with this owner, so felt comfortable having a discussion with him about stepping into the role as manager of the smaller property, just south of Elliott. This wasn't part of the owner's plan but he did tell us that there was another place coming up nearby, as the manager was retiring to concentrate on his fledgling trucking business. That he was on good terms with the Trustees who administered this property and if Mick was interested, he would recommend him for the post.

Mick was duly interviewed by the board of Trustees, his current position and prior experience in the industry together with a strong recommendation was deemed sufficient to appoint him as the new manager of Beetaloo Station. The Employment Contract was drawn up and together with all the promises made, was duly signed. Mick resigned his position with the AIB and at the end of the year we packed our belongings, ready to start the new role at the beginning of 1970. We weren't moving far, Mick had been working with the people and manager of Beetaloo as it was part of the Elliott district, he knew the country, was familiar with the breed of cattle and knew the history of the property. Which was an interesting story in itself.

There are 2 stories to tell now, one is a short history of Beetaloo Station, the other is about a person who had played a big part in our lives from the first day we arrived in Elliott and Mick took over the district.

I'll tell you about 'Whitefoot' first. Whitefoot; to the best of my knowledge was a Jingili man. The Jingili region lies in the central section of the Barkly district, it centres around Elliott and Newcastle Waters and encompasses the outlying areas of Daly Waters to the north, and Renner Springs to the south. I never knew him by any other name, we think that he was given that name due to a burn scar on his leg. He was employed by the AIB as Dip Attendant, so was Mick's right-hand man, he went most places with Mick, when I went along, he would ride on the back of the vehicle. Mick and he often camped out together. Sometimes Whitefoot stayed at the house with me and cut wood or did gardening, though mostly he went with Mick, to Top Springs or Timber Creek and surrounding properties TB testing, inspecting stock routes and checking feed cover, meeting drovers on the way to Elliott. Going out to stations that had dips where the cattle needed to be inspected prior to travelling, or checking the waters along the Murranji and Barkly Stock Routes.

He and Mick were good mates and he was a friend to me. If he happened to be at the house, we'd have smoko or lunch together and he'd tell me about his life and ask questions about mine, he'd keep an eye on Brenton if I was hanging out laundry. He never missed a day at work, if he was ill Mick would have to take him home and tell him to rest up and get better. He couldn't read but liked to look at the pictures in newspapers, asking me what it was all about. When his wife died, he came to work with tears running down his cheeks. Mick, knowing the customs of the Indigenous people, took his hand and told him to go walk-about for as long as he needed. He just nodded and walked off. I don't remember how long he was gone but one evening he came by the house with a live goanna tied around his leg, goanna stays fresh that way 'til you're ready to cook it, he explained to me and announced he was back and would come to work the next day.

Sometime later he and Mick headed off as usual, up the Murranji to Wave Hill. Mick later told me there was quite a welcome committee when they arrived, not for him but for Whitefoot. It was time for him to be given a new wife. This time a young one, Emily had been his same age wife, he explained that man and woman usually had 3 partners. As a young person you had the responsibility of caring for an older wife, then you had same age wife for a family, your final wife was young so she could take care of you. I later witnessed the same system at work on Beetaloo Station. The further revelation on this trip was that Whitefoot was an esteemed Elder and spokesperson for his people. He bore the tribal markings of initiation. He was one of life's true gentlemen. It was a privilege to have known him.

The story of Beetaloo Station: an abridged version. This cattle station came into being in the 1890s when Harry Bathern, a drover, was granted a grazing lease over that area of traditional land. The Indigenous owners being the Jingili people. Harry Bathern had partners in this enterprise, two Bostock brothers and Will Miller. These men together with the assistance of the traditional owners, built houses, stock yards, sheds and fences. Put down bores and erected windmills to water the livestock further away from the Newcastle Creek which ran through the property. They raised cattle and horses; the horses were renowned for their quality and were sought after as remounts for the Indian Army Campaigns. They cleared the timber and put in an airstrip so that the Flying Doctor could land in an emergency. The outstation of OT Downs was developed by one of the Bostock brothers and Will Miller. They married local women and had families; the children became the heirs to the property which was administered through a Trust set up by the partners to secure a future for their descendants. It was a vast holding, three and a half thousand square miles, comprising a variety of terrains from heavily timbered 'Lancewood' country to open grassland.

The traditional owners were still living on the property alongside the heirs when we came to manage the cattle enterprise. Two separate living areas were established, one for the traditional owners and one for the families. Up on a rise overlooking the billabong were a row of cottages for the families. A saddle house and machinery shed were part of the early buildings.

Later more living quarters were added with a large communal kitchen and an apartment for the 'cook'. A second building of similar size housed the school room, station store, office and Managers accommodation. There was another smaller building fitted out with ablution facilities and laundry near the Managers accommodation and a meat-house. Water was pumped into an overhead tank from the billabong to supply everyone and there was a generator to supply lighting to the entire complex, 32volt no 240volt, fridges were kerosene or LPG gas. There was no cool room, just the 'meat house and a small meat-safe'.

The village for the Aboriginal people consisted of one newer building similar size to the single men's quarters, also divided into rooms and a communal kitchen, ablution facilities shared by 3 or 4 families and a collection of huts for pensioners. These huts were old but in good condition, single room with a verandah, much like the building on Coburg Peninsula where we started our married life together.

The 'Williams Hut' came in all sizes, from tiny huts to aircraft hangers, corrugated iron and steel, could be delivered flat and erected on site without too much trouble. Prior to that the buildings were bush timber framed and corrugated iron clad. Some of the earlier ones had rammed earth floors, the newer ones were built on concrete slabs. None of them were lined internally. Harry Bathern died in 1928 and is buried on a hill overlooking the station buildings, alongside him lay buried his two partners, the Bostock brothers. Mick placed the headstones to mark their graves in 1970.

**

Managing the Station

In 1970 we began the next stage of our lives on Beetaloo Station. Mick now officially appointed, the Manager. For me it was another new beginning with new challenges. I was grateful that we'd bought the caravan; it was so civilised and almost luxurious inside compared to the rudimentary accommodation provided by the station. We'd been promised that a kit home would be built for us within the year, a new Toyota and a station truck came but no kit home. It was so very hot that summer, I lost weight instead of gaining it during my pregnancy.

Whitefoot had decided to quit his job with the AIB, he didn't want to start over with yet another stock inspector, preferring to stay with Mick and came out to Beetaloo as well. He was just as much at home there as he was in Elliott; he didn't bring his new wife; he only brought his swag and his dogs; living on traditional lands with his people suited him well.

Mick set to work, he assessed the situation and made a list of priorities. High on the agenda was to complete the stockyards and new dip, so that the frantic occurrence of the previous year, when I took Brenton to Alice Springs could be avoided. The cattle could now be clean dipped at the property and trucked direct to points of sale, without the double handling and the need to spell them at the Number 7 dip between treatments. Next the fencing of the new paddocks needed to be completed, the new style of fencing was called suspension fencing. It was much quicker to put up, used less material, and in the event of cattle rushing for any reason it stood back up and required less maintenance than traditional fencing. There were two bores to equip and windmills to erect, he opted for mono pumps; windmills were traditionally equipped with bucket pumps, a cylinder with a series of internal diaphragms. Mono pumps work on a screw principal, provide a consistent flow rate, are self-priming and require less overall maintenance.

The horse muster came next, the horse books were updated and the ledgers filled out. Cattle were mustered, branded and drafted into paddocks. Weaners separated, the store cattle put into separate paddocks, the bulls ran with the herd year-round so there was no set calving season. There were large sections of the property which were heavily timbered and the cattle were free range, so consequently wild. The only way to get them out was with lures like salt licks. Mick ordered salt, built hessian yards with wide wings and loading ramps, the cattle mustered themselves going in for the licks. Once they had become accustomed to the routine it was time to shut the gate on them. The stockmen camped nearby. Once the gate was shut the truck was brought in and the cattle loaded. Many were clean skins; they hadn't been branded or handled in any way. The only place for them to go was to Katherine, direct to the abattoir due to the ticks. Mick was to receive a $1 bonus per head for every one sold this way. A lot of effort went into sorting out the herd. Mick had 3 stock camps set up, 2 on Beetaloo and one on OT Downs. His time spent between all three. Every able-bodied stockman was working. The mechanic was kept busy too, doing the water runs, checking the windmills and cleaning troughs.

Brenton and I went with Mick whenever it was practical, sometimes up to OT Downs, sometimes to check on the stock camps, we camped out if we were too far away from the station. Most of the time I stayed at the station looking after things there, manning the store, handing out rations, keeping up the bookwork and tracking the payroll. Cooking and baking bread, the rations we had were rather poor and meagre. The flour was full of weevils, the powdered milk so stale it wouldn't stay in suspension. There were never enough potatoes or onions, nor pumpkins. What we did get was stored on wire racks between layers of hessian, in the meat house. The vegetables wilted in the heat and didn't keep very well. So; we relied on canned or dehydrated vegetables or what we could grow ourselves.

The station supplied the meat, generally 2 beasts per week, there were a lot of mouths to feed. Fresh meat only kept a few days hanging up on hooks, so most of the meat was salted down in coarse salt and air dried. There was a fair bit of traditional food being cooked down in the village, you could smell the singed fur and see the odd set of hoppers being dragged about by the dogs. When the flour got so bad that the weevils had eaten out all the nourishment, our bread turned into a crust with a mud spring in the centre, we made damper which wasn't much better or johnny cakes. We were all in the same situation, no favouritism. The Bathern women became my companions, they'd call on me and we'd compare our baking disasters and drink tea together. We met in the meat-house and shared the vegetables and meat; they would help unpack and load the store when the truck arrived. We'd chat about our children and watch them play together in the red earth under the overhanging roof.

I was able to treat the everyday ills and injuries, falling back on my limited nursing training and the flying doctor medical chest. There was a bout of impetigo among the children, highly infectious so it spread rapidly. We held a daily clinic to bathe and treat the sores until everyone was clear. Then there were nits, so again the treatments began. We also had a run of ringworm, lots of purple paint and antifungal ointment. A few cuts and bruises but nothing too serious. Just one nasty accident, one of the stockmen was thrown from his horse and had concussion, the plane had to come for him. The airstrip was a bit short; the planes were bigger now. Signal fires were lit and the smoke guided the pilot in against the wind, our patient was loaded and the plane took off, just skimming the top of the trees as he gained altitude.

Lengthening the airstrip was a job for another day. Once a month or so the district nurse managed to call out to us on her rounds. I wasn't the only expectant mother.

We had quite a few visitors out to the station. Stock agents lining up sale dates, salesmen trying to sell everything from heavy machinery to tools, and the Aboriginal Welfare Officer, with his help we were able to secure a pension for Whitefoot so that he had an income. Our souls were also being taken care of by visiting clergy. Never a dull moment, always someone looking for a smoko, lunch or dinner.

The best of all was a team of painters. The station buildings needed sprucing up, the village got a coat of whitewash over the walls and silver-frost on the roofs. All the older buildings looked good; the newer ones were still okay. I'm not sure if the pensioners were all that pleased, most of them slept out for a few days. Beetaloo was what was known as a DRY station, no alcohol allowed past the boundary gate. If you wanted a drink you had to go to town, so there was a regular convoy into town on Friday and back on Sunday afternoon. There wasn't any trouble on the station as a result, no fights, just a few arguments now and then. It was mainly peaceful.

The schoolmaster, who had been there for a number of years tendered his resignation, then left in the next vehicle going to town. This caused considerable upset among the people, there were about 10 permanent school aged children and numbers were often boosted by visiting families. The Trustees advertised for a replacement. The governess with her young son arrived a few weeks later, she moved into the bedroom reserved for our use, sharing the kitchen and living room. We continued to sleep in our caravan. Classes resumed soon afterwards; the younger children had a new playmate. Then it was time for me to go to Darwin, baby was due any day now, I had a friend from nursing days I could stay with. Mick took me into Elliot to catch the bus, Brenton stayed with his father. Within the week Brenton had a brother, our son Paul Leonard Bailey was born on 29th June 1970. Named after both his grandfathers.

My best friend from nursing days (my bridesmaid) was in the same ward, her daughter was born the next day. It was lovely to reconnect. She'd been living in Canberra with her husband and he'd recently been transferred back to Darwin. Mick came up to collect us, Brenton met his brother, he wasn't terribly interested in him yet but he'd enjoyed being a big boy and travelling around the station with his father during my absence. It was winter, the dry season, so Paul got to use the nice warm baby clothes that we'd been sent for Brenton.

Whitefoot was there to greet us and welcome our new son. He'd made totems for him, a coolamon for him to sleep in, (a safe place) a boomerang, shaped from the root and trunk of a Bullwaddy tree and wooden spear carved from a lancewood tree and a stone axe head. All decorated with ochre, tribal symbols depicting a white child, to help him on his journey through life. I was speechless, it was such a beautiful gesture, a gift from one culture to another. A coolamon is a canoe shaped bowl cut from the side of a hard-wood tree, it was used by the women when out gathering, to carry items of food, usually carried on the head. It was also used to carry their babies in, balanced on the hip.

Whitefoot travelled around the station with Mick most days, showed him secret places, where grind stones were hidden among thickets of Bullwaddy trees. These large flat stones have a circular depression made by a smaller round stone and are used to grind seeds, bulbs and berries. Too heavy to carry when following the seasons, they are hidden until the next time they were needed, also where they got stone tips for spears and knives used for cutting and hunting. The old saying of 'seek and you shall find', is befitting, but you do need to know where to look.

Mick worked extremely hard to bring together the massive task he'd set himself. I still went with him whenever it seemed practical. When we camped out, Brenton had his own swag, our dogs (Lady and Sue) slept one each side of him, preventing him from rolling out, for Paul we had a bush cradle, a calico sling with enclosed ends, slung between two sets of crossed legs. It looked a bit like a clothes airer with a mozzie net over it. Rustic but very serviceable.

One night I was woken by scratching on the side of the caravan, a whispered distress call from one of the Aboriginal women. A woman was in labour, she'd had 3 previous babies, the last one was complicated, she'd bled heavily. I had discussed this case with the district nurse who had calculated an approximate due date, so this child was coming early. God help me, I hadn't had any experience delivering a baby. I'd spent a brief time in the labour ward assisting but was no midwife. I went down to the camp and tried to make the woman comfortable, checked how far she was along in the labour, it wouldn't be long. The Aboriginal women who were attending her were re-assured, they knew what to do now. Nature took over and the child was born, no complications, a very tired mother and a tiny baby girl. Everyone felt relieved, now able to go to bed.

Next morning, I went and checked on her and the baby, it was very small. We got in touch with the Flying Doctor and were told she and the child needed to go to Tennant Creek to hospital for a proper checkup, her husband wasn't happy about it at all, Tennant Creek was south of traditional land. After much discussion it was agreed that she could go as long as the midwife and an auntie could go too, one of the other families would look after the older two children, the youngest one would go with them. It takes a village, there were plenty of helpers and child minding was organised. Her husband could go back out to the stock-camp. He was one of the head stockmen, before he rode out, he put on his new white Stetson and wore a big smile.

Brenton gave us the fright of our lives the day he went missing. The homestead area was surrounded by a horse paddock and at one end was the Newcastle Creek. The paddock was dry, a few stunted trees and scant grass, some scraggly bushes, the goats had eaten it bare. It was ochre coloured and stony. Words of warning echoed around in my head. A woman had warned me to never let him wear shoes. She had lost a child who had wandered off. We raised the alarm, everyone stopped what they were doing and went to search in all directions, little feet didn't leave much of a track to follow, after a heart stopping time that felt like hours he was spotted, the dogs were with him. He hadn't gone to the water; he was following a baby goat that had caught his attention. We were so relieved. His tan made him the same colour as the surrounding country and his hair was so fair. If he hadn't crossed in front of a dark wrecked car the outcome could have been too unthinkable to contemplate. He wasn't wearing shoes, his feet had hardened from walking around barefoot, so he could walk around on hot earth and stones without any trouble at all, all he had on was a pair of tan shorts.

As the year progressed it started to become clear that the employment contract wasn't going to be honoured. There was no sign of the promised home. When Mick asked about it, he was told perhaps next year, things were tight. Then there was a dispute over the bonus that was to be paid for the cattle that were turned off. Mick told the trustees he would stay until the end of the year, giving them time to find a replacement manager, that also gave us time to pack up and make plans.

Our dogs couldn't come with us into such an uncertain future, Lady was an old girl now and Sue was a working cattle dog. They went to live on a neighbouring property with friends, we were assured they would be safe and well looked after. Whitefoot moved back into town, he still had his house in the village. There were a few long faces when we hooked up the caravan and said our farewells. It was a solemn leave taking. Looking back Mick had left the place in better shape than when we arrived, we'd made a difference, it was better for everyone on Beetaloo Station, better pay, better food, better conditions but we didn't feel like rejoicing.

With two cats and two children we headed back up the Stuart Highway towards Darwin, we booked into the caravan park in Katherine that night, our ginger cat went missing. We waited three days, he didn't come back, so we had no option but to carry on without him. We still had the calico cat. When we reached Darwin, we booked into a caravan park by the beach and became part of a sub-culture.

Darwin had changed, hippies now lived on Lamaroo Beach in tree houses.

The last few years had certainly been a time of change;

- 1966 The Wave Hill strike; it lasted 7 years, all the people wanted was a fair deal and to live on their traditional lands. They had to wait until 1975 before they got legal title to their lands. Wally Bathern had the foresight to set up the Trust and make provision for his descendants and their people.
- 1967; The referendum carried and the Constitution was changed. Aboriginal and Torres Strait Islander people would be counted as part of the population and the Commonwealth would be able to make laws for them.
- 1968 Lionel Rose, the Aboriginal boxing champion was named Australian of the Year.
- 1969 the Arbitration Court ruled that equal pay for women doing the same work as men must be phased in by 1972.
- 1970 the "Time for Change" protest demonstrations, opposition against conscription and the Vietnam War reached its peak with a national moratorium.

Barbara was now quite grown up had graduated from high school.

***

Settling Down - Who does that?

Darwin, just in time for another wet season, incessant rain and high humidity, everything damp and clammy, two small children in a

4.5 x 2.5m caravan, divided in half to form two small roomettes. We didn't have an annex so our boxed belongings were under beds, or under the van trying to keep them dry. Maximum stay time at this park was three months. We had a nice car but not much else.

Mick registered with a hire car company as a driver, our family car became a 'Hire Car', it was a white 1968 model V8 Valiant Sedan. The company took a percentage of the takings in exchange for the license to operate under their name. The proprietor was known as "The Pieman", he took a slice from every pie. Mick was working nights and trying to sleep during the day. We used part of our savings to install a small air-conditioning unit to make it bearable inside. I took the children out whenever there was a break in the weather, the park was full of families in similar circumstances. The housing situation in Darwin hadn't improved. We made friends easily and supported each other as best we could.

My grandmother died that year; she was on the other side of the world. I hadn't seen her since I was a small child but we had written letters and she sent the most wonderful parcels full of treats and presents for our birthdays and at Christmas. Not this year though, my family was very sad, especially mother. My parents sent us a cheque to buy Christmas presents for the children, we spent the money on food for a Christmas dinner, not on toys. Brenton dropped most of his down the storm drains when they were running, then raced to the beach to see if any came out the other end, some did - a lot didn't. Paul was just a baby, happy to play with pot lids and wooden spoons. The rest of the toys were packed up under the van going mouldy along with everything else. Our treasures and wedding gifts were boxed up and stayed under our bed.

In the summer of '69 I had stuck flowers onto the back of the van, the park children worked hard and managed to pull most of them off, I was more than a little upset. They found a can of paint from somewhere, black enamel, Brenton became the 'Tar Baby'. We both cried as I cleaned it off his delicate skin, fortunately he'd had shorts on, and they hadn't painted his face or hair. My friend was expecting a baby, the child was stillborn. She was treated appallingly by the hospital system, no counselling, minimal aftercare for her, just heart-break for her husband. She leaned on me and I tried to comfort her as best I could, we cried together more than once. Her little daughter, same age as Brenton didn't understand why mother was so sad, it was awful for all of them. They did their best to get through the tragedy but it left a terrible scar. We remained friends for a long time, but eventually drifted apart.

Our three months was up, we had to look for another place to park the van, there weren't any vacancies in any of the other registered parks, but the backyards in Darwin were a good size, so some enterprising people turned their homes into boarding houses and filled their backyards with three or four caravans. Our van made number four, power was via extension cords draped through tree branches, the single outside ablution facility was run on a roster system, our laundry lines tied to tree branches made a good ant highway. One had to be careful taking in the washing.

No point complaining, although I was feeling particularly low one day and rang mother, she told me to "toughen up, at least we weren't at war!" just as the monthly air raid sirens were being tested, a relic from the Japanese attack from WWII. Sometimes the ridiculous will put it all into perspective. Our neighbour in the next van was a single mother of seven children. Her eldest daughter had a babe in arms. Their van was the same size as ours but had a tarpaulin tied on one side, how they all fitted is a mystery to this day. She was the happiest person I knew then, with a positive sunny view of the world. She made me realise again that we all could have fun and still be happy with very little. Paul had a lovely first birthday party in the garden, all the children joining in for sweets and cake.

Our name finally came up at the best caravan park in town, our site was one of the few that had a private bathroom, not the usual shared facilities. We were very pleased to be going there, yet sad to leave the little community we were a part of. Meanwhile Mick's parents had moved to Darwin from Port Moresby and Mick had, through contacts, got them a house down at Batchelor. Strange folk his parents, they were ashamed that we were living in a caravan and would stop at the roadhouse opposite our caravan park for refreshments, rather than visit us in the van. Yet we were expected to go to them whenever beckoned. I still shake my head about that attitude.

Our calico cat went missing, she was due to have kittens and must have made a nest somewhere safe, but she never came back. Finally, a stroke of real luck. Mick's fare to pick up people from the 'Dog-track' (Greyhound races) one Friday evening just happened to be his old boss from the AIB and the new Director. Best news yet, they were recruiting and Mick was offered his old position. He was elated when he got home that night. The following Monday all the formalities were taken care of and he was reinstated by the end of the month. 'The Pieman' arranged a very nice send-off for Mick, at a restaurant on the other side of Darwin Harbour which included a harbour cruise. I celebrated a little too much and was quite ill on the way back.

One of the first things that Mick did when he started back with the AIB was to adopt a cat for me, she had been handed in at the department, a stray with a litter of kittens, abandoned when her people left and the new tenant didn't want her. His friend, one of the vets, operated to spey her after work on his office desk. She was still groggy when Mick brought her home. By the time she fully recovered from the anaesthetic she was our cat. She never had a name other than 'Puss-cat'. The boys and I were very happy to have her, that little calico cat lived with us for the next 19 years.

Our lucky star continued to shine on us and Mick was sent to Batchelor as meat inspector at the local abattoir. We had a furnished house again. The old mining town had been taken over by the NT Administration and was being repurposed. The Rum Jungle uranium mine had closed down a few years earlier. Another community to settle into and new people to meet and befriend. 1971 certainly had shown us a different side of life.

It was lovely down at Batchelor, a little town surrounded by the tropical jungle, full of nature, creeks, myriad of under-story plants, orchids high in the trees, birds, flying foxes, insects and animals. The town had avenues of mature mango trees, hibiscus and frangipani, huge poinciana and Golden Rain trees, lawns, no fences, just hedges of colourful tropical shrubs. Mick's parents lived at one end of the street; we were at the other. They had a 2-bedroom high-set house, room for outdoor living and car parking underneath, ours had 3-bedrooms. Again, fully furnished, the furniture wasn't new but it was serviceable. Were we settling down? My new friend was an American lady married to a Canadian geologist, she had a little boy Paul's age and was expecting a baby. Her husband was away doing field work and she was lonely and homesick, missing everything familiar. They had come to Australia from Alaska so you can imagine the culture shock she was experiencing. We spent quite a lot of time together.

We gave Brenton a 'tractor' pedal car that Christmas and Paul a ride-on toy with handlebars, two happy little boys. Christmas lunch was planned to be with Mick's parents, we had hidden the toys at their house, so were there for breakfast as well. Mick's father had bought a camphor wood engraved chest for me before he left New Guinea, his parents gave it to me that year. It was a beautiful piece and I used it to store my mementos for years to come. Brenton had coveted that tractor from the first time he saw it in the toyshop window, many tantrums ensued each time we passed the shop, he couldn't believe his eyes that Christmas morning, he was so eager to start riding it he pushed it down the stairs, we all held our breath, it was a sturdy toy and passed the test

The wet ended and Mick started to go bush again, the boys and I went with him whenever we could, still camping out under the stars. Mick's mother didn't approve, accused me of 'playing at marriage and motherhood'. Mick and I loved our togetherness and didn't care much for convention, it didn't hurt the boys to be free spirits either. We were a close family and did everything together. Once when the children and I were with him, as Mick was closing up the abattoir at the end of the day, the door jammed and kicked back onto his foot, tearing his toenail away from the nailbed. He had only just taken off the gum boots and put thongs on. He had to suffer my driving the vehicle back to town, the nail was unceremoniously removed by the doctor and the wound dressed.

Mick was on desk duties now, so was able to take us to the Adelaide River Agricultural Show. At sideshow alley there were the usual tricks and entertainment, the' hit the button and see how high the meter went up the scale' was a popular one, so Mick decided to show his ability to the boys, not a good idea; the hammer rebound whacked him on his damaged foot, he fell back in pain into a pile of empty boxes. What does one do in such a circumstance, laugh or cry! the boys laughed, he almost cried, I packed the three of them up and drove them home.

By now I was much more confident about driving on unmade roads in the bush so I decided to take the children out to visit Mick in our most 'unsuitable for the terrain and road conditions' family car. Our nice new red Renault. The main hazard being the bull dust patches we had to get through. When the black soil plains dry out the vehicle traffic turns the clay soil into the finest talc like dust, the dust often hiding deep wheel ruts made during the wet season. No matter, the car was light enough to push out if we got stuck and there was a lot more traffic out there on the plains now to assist a damsel in distress. We had only been there for a couple of days when we got a telegram to tell us that my mother was staying with Mick's parents, she was most displeased that her welcome committee hadn't been there to greet her.

A hasty return needed to be made, Mick was due to go back to town shortly, the abattoir owner was okay about closing until Mick's relief would arrive. A radio call to head office and the relief inspector was on the way out. We headed back, me in the lead, with Mick following in case I got stuck. No dramas but the rub marks from the dust had permanently etched the windows, I'd had them partly rolled down as the car didn't have air-conditioning and we never were quite able to get all the fine dust out of the cabin. Fortunately, I had kept the letter where mother advised us her arrival date, she was only a month early. Egg on her face.

Shortly after Christmas 1971 our name came up for a house in Darwin, a brand-new concrete tilt-panel construction, an experimental building style being tried in the Territory for the first time. A three-bedroom high-set house on a bare block in a brand-new subdivision. The landscape of shiny roofs, hardly a tree left standing. We moved in, it was barren ground, all the topsoil had been scraped away. Mick brought in loads of good soil and we planted a garden. A good thing about the tropics is that if you put a stick into the ground it will grow. We took a lot of sticks up from Batchelor, cuttings from all those colourful shrubs and soon had lawns and hedges to hide the cyclone wire fencing.

Mick planted a front hedge, it must have been a carnivorous plant, he'd feed it with 'blood-n-bone' it would grow then wilt, he repeated the cycle over and over. It never stopped being hungry. I planted two Singapore Orchid trees on the verge, Mick planted an Indian Almond tree in the middle of the front lawn. We planted the most exotic tropical garden with bananas, breadfruit, tropical peach and Mahogany trees, bougainvillea and other climbers. I'd say we had the nicest garden in the shortest time in the whole suburb.

Brenton started school in February, it was an open plan 'new age' experimental school. The educational facilitators (we used to call them teachers) had rather radical ideas in their approach. Brenton spent first term out in the school playground, mainly riding around on his scooter. We queried why he wasn't in class with the others doing what first year children did, we were assured he would come in when he felt he was ready. Not convinced we moved him to a small private, more conventional school in the next suburb. He was now being taught the fundamentals of literacy and numeracy and was still allowed to play games. We felt the move had been a success.

The dry season came and Mick was going bush again, starting the rotational change of three weeks out and one week back in town. The inspectors were also rotated to different locations routinely, last year he'd been mainly in Arnhem Land at various buffalo abattoirs, one of which was Woolwonga Reserve. Traditional land of the Wulwulam people, on the banks of the Alligator River, (now Kakadu National Park) also at others on the Marrakai Plains, where I had first met him. The history of the Northern Territory is an amazing story in itself, and if your interest lies in that direction, the places I mention in my story will come up in detail if you look for them on-line. Oenpelli (Gunbalanya) across the East Alligator River, a place that would fill a chapter to describe, so beautiful with magnificent waters covered in lotus, vast plains rich with wildlife, escarpments with cascading waterfalls, I could go on for pages.

I was blessed to have experienced and seen so much of it. The beauty not without peril. When we were at Oenpelli the boys had decided to follow Mick down to the abattoir, I was busy tidying the camp after lunch, these two boys could move like lightening. I looked up to witness a heart stopping scene unfold. Two little boys walking down the track, the buffalo in the yards broke free, one of the workers was running to snatch the children out of harm's way. Time seemed to stand still. He had saved my children at considerable risk to himself, a true hero. He was a missionary at Oenpelli, there with his family, working to establish the meat works so that economic development would ultimately benefit the Indigenous people. There were other initiatives underway as well, the buffalo horns were being carved into artefacts, or mounted as wall ornaments, sought after by the increasing tourist trade.

With Brenton now in school my visits were curtailed to school breaks. I was left at home, so interior décor became my focus, the psychedelic era of the '70's. I painted and wallpapered, made curtains, we purchased furniture of our own, returning the rented items bit by bit. The house was on a rent to buy contract, and the furniture was rented as well. We had air-conditioning installed, had a pool put in, upset the neighbours by installing high pool fencing, told them that if they wanted to have the children use the pool, they had to be with them and supervise them. Friendly relations were restored.

We traded our caravan and purchased a boat, or rather a series of boats. First a dingy with an outboard motor, then a power boat with a bigger motor, which was soon followed by a half cabin bigger boat, suitable for open water with a fuel guzzling bigger again motor. Previously we only cruised around the harbour. Our boating misadventures could fill a volume. We didn't catch many fish or crabs; Brenton caught the biggest one on his little rod. We ran into tropical storms and came out by the very skin of our teeth, almost lost the boat when high tide came in, leaving us stranded on a beach. Good thing Mick was a strong swimmer, he managed to get on board and start the engine and raise the anchor before it sank. We were better on dry land. I'll curtail the story here; the last boat was sold before the year was out.

Another year had passed, another dry season began meaning more trips away for Mick, posted to both beef and buffalo abattoirs doing meat inspection. The stock inspectors in the NT wore many hats, they were gazetted as Stock, Meat, Fisheries, Quarantine and Bush Fire Inspectors, and Wildlife Rangers. A man for any occasion and they could be called on at any time to fulfil any of these roles, sometimes more than one concurrently. Stationed at McArthur River, Wild-Boar, Menling, the list goes on.

The visit to McArthur River is a stand-out; the children and I rode down in the delivery truck to the station during term break, our driver sported a luxurious beard, his name started with H, the children figured his name must have been Hairy, so Hairy was what he answered to. The station was set up like a small town, as most of them were. Quarters for everyone including the mess hut with an outdoor beer garden area, seating was on log stools. The boys managed to roll them all down the hill and into the lagoon, I was told not to reprimand them; the staff thought it was nice to see such free spirits. A spotter plane from the gulf prawn fishing industry came in and exchanged cartons of prawns for fresh meat, everyone enjoyed the change of diet. As this was a working cattle station as well as having its own abattoir, cattle work went on alongside the meat processing.

Helicopter mustering was new, 'choppers managed to drive cattle out of timbered areas where men on horseback had difficulty, but once the mob were in the open could take control, yard them and do the rest, McArthur River used 'choppers. The boys and I were invited to go for a fly, we had the best scenic flight over the station and down through the McArthur River Gorge. It was exhilarating, a wonderful experience. The staff on cattle properties were always an interesting group of people who came from many different walks of life. The station had been purchased by an American company, they employed a number of American Vietnam veterans. Australia was their new horizon, attracting them, just as it had previous generations looking for a fresh start and adventure.

Wild Boar Abattoir was much closer to Darwin, so easier for me to get to. We stayed out there for the next school break. The boys had a wonderful time, other children to play with, a pet baby buffalo to ride and a tame wedgetail eagle which had been hand raised. All of the children grew up with free spirits. The staff again a diverse group of people, some hippy drifters who spent their free time looking for magic mushrooms, then regaling tales of their hallucinations around the campfire in the evenings, others came from the Torres Strait Islands and as far away as New Zealand.

Competition was fierce on the slaughter floor, it was who could skin a beast in the fastest time, in the boning room who could remove the bones in record time, in the packing room who could pack the most cartons, all good natured, but the occasional accident resulted, deep cuts from very sharp knives the most common. Meat inspection also required the use of sharp knives and Mick was not immune from injury. He sustained a particularly nasty cut to one of his thumbs, cutting through the nerve and main blood vessel. He had to keep his arm elevated so we could get the bleeding under control and the wound dressed. No sutures, just pressure until the bleeding was stemmed. The wound healed but the nerve didn't, his thumb remained without feeling for years.

I got bored sitting at home with Mick away for most of the year. The time he was away seemed longer every month. That year he just made it home for Christmas, the wet season was late starting so the meat-works extended operations, then the storms came in with a rush. The rivers flooded and the exodus began, people were stranded on the wrong side of the rivers, waiting for tidal change so they could cross. No bridges then, just low level stony crossings. A truck was going through and Mick was next, attached to the back of the truck staying in the wake. The river was too fast and the vehicle too light, it rolled, Mick managed to squeeze out of the window and get on-top of the vehicle, they reached the other side. The flooded vehicle was righted, water drained, fresh oil and fuel and he was mobile again and drove home.

He arrived late that night. I was shocked to see him looking so dishevelled, sporting a full beard and a black eye, filthy dirty into the bargain. Shock soon turned to utter relief when he'd showered and told me of his misadventure. The boys were delighted to see him next morning. Another problem with the increasing absences was that it was having an impact on the children. How do you explain to little boys sitting forlornly on the steps that dad will be home in X number of sleeps, when they refuse to come inside at dusk because dad isn't home yet, then when he was at home and asked them to come or do something, have them asking him if 'mum said'. Certainly not ideal.

The separation from his family was also hard on Mick, said he didn't get married and have a family to spend so much time away from us. It was lonely, especially in the evenings and at night after the day's work was done and the workers on stations or aboriginal missions went home to their families. His accommodation was usually a small hut or caravan, with stand-alone ablution facilities, sometimes as rudimentary as a bough shed covered with a tarpaulin, furnished with a single chair and a cyclone 'shearers' bed to lay his swag on. His vehicle was relatively well kitted out with camping equipment, he cooked on an open fire, using his billycan, camp oven or a small hotplate set on inverted horseshoes, fresh water in jerrycans. The back of the vehicle his kitchen bench. He carried supplies with him and his tucker-box was well stocked, fresh meat was always available. Some of the larger places had a communal kitchen for single personnel to eat meals, but even there he often chose to cater for himself.

On his return from one of his trips to Oenpelli he told me that one evening the pastor had come to his camp for the evening to pass the time. The conversation had led to Mick's concerns about being away from family, his time alone making him think about the future, how he could best provide for his family and leave his sons a legacy, a financial start in life and a secure future for us once age led to retirement. Worrying that his lack of formal education and the nomadic lifestyle he had chosen from a young age making it difficult to fit into the competitive world we were now living in. This weighed heavy on his mind, the pastor reminded him that he was only human, could only do his best with the skills he had, that his responsibility as a husband and father was to love his family, do all he could to keep a roof over their heads, food on the table and ensure that his sons got the best education that he could provide. Once they reached maturity, they would find their own way in the world and live their lives, Mick's duty was not to amass a fortune to pave an easy path for them to follow, they had their natural ability and freedom of choice to succeed in their chosen endeavour, just as he was doing at this very time.

Someone like this pastor connecting with you at a vulnerable time in your life feels like a divine act, heaven sent to ally your fears and to give you the fortitude and guidance to continue on your journey with a knowledge that you will be alright. When Mick told me about this evening I was overcome with emotion, realising again how much he cared for us and tried to reassure him that I similarly would work alongside him to ensure that our little family would succeed along life's journey no matter where it would take us.

Barbara was an adult now working as an air hostess with Ansett Airlines. She would visit whenever possible during a layover in Darwin, though often she only had a short turn-around. I was always overjoyed to see her, I had missed her more than I can say through the years, so much I had wanted to share with her. Mother came to visit also, I didn't understand why she would always start off with an unpleasant attitude, once she was so unbearable that Mick told her he would ring his mate who managed one of the airlines to get her on the next plane home. She retorted very indignantly, that she had come a long way to visit her daughter and that she would be staying put. She rarely referred to me by name, I was always 'her daughter' or my child. So, stay she did and suddenly her attitude did a U-turn and it was a pleasure to have her with us.

Father changed employment again, no more visits from him on State Ships. He was back on the east coast on the survey ships, his relationship with mother had been fragile for years, his long absences also taking a toll on their marriage. Mother was still working at all sorts of menial jobs, she hadn't been able to secure a secretarial position yet, but was involved in the German *Rhein Donau* Club, she had friends there and it eased her loneliness. I had also started working outside the home, a part-time position during school hours. Paul was at day-care which took half of my earnings, but it helped me through Mick's stints away.

Shortly before Christmas 1974 we went south for a holiday to Adelaide to do our Christmas shopping. The boys hadn't been to a big city toy department store before, a visit to the Santa Cave at Myers was an adventure, they saw and wanted toy swords, Mick purchased a couple and hid them under his coat, the tantrum on the way out of the store was extreme, it drew quite a crowd, the children were not going to leave without a sword each; in order to placate them Mick had no option but to hand them over. The crowd of onlookers who had gathered to witness the tantrums dispersed with smiles on their faces.

Later that day when we were back at our hotel, Mick had to stay very calm and persuade our 'Musketeers' to get down from the balcony balustrade on the 4th floor of the hotel and come back inside.

While we were on our way back to the Territory a savage storm was impacting Darwin. Our flight was diverted to Mount Isa, after a short delay we were told we could fly into Darwin after all. As we approached the city the captain had to circle the plane to burn fuel prior to landing, Cyclone "Selma" had narrowly bypassed Darwin delivering 80km winds and heavy rain; it had been a bumpy ride. On arriving home, we found our new carpets wet, the rain had driven under the door weather seals. Never could we have imagined what was in store just a few weeks later.

***

Cyclone Tracy wasn't the first cyclone to have a devastating effect on Darwin. Darwin had been hit by numerous cyclones and suffered significant damage in the past, many of its citizens losing their lives to natural disaster and during the bombings in WWII. The spirit of the population and their resilience triumphed over all these setbacks and the town grew into a city

Long before cyclones were named; in 1897 when the population of Darwin was about 1300 an extremely destructive cyclone hit the town, twenty-eight souls lost their lives, for a long time the town lay in ruins, the South Australian Government showing little commitment to rebuild Darwin and scars of that cyclone were still visible when the Commonwealth took control of the Northern Territory in 1911. There were further cyclones but the next one in 1937 caused loss of life and a lot of damage to the town, official records indicate it was much milder than Tracy.

Just five years later in 1942 Darwin was bombed by Japanese aircraft, this attack wrought enormous destruction and fatalities.

In December 2004 the Northern Territory News printed a series of supplements for the 30th anniversary of the night Cyclone Tracy wrought its destruction on the city of Darwin, Christine (our daughter-in-law) was able to obtain copies for us; on reading through them I think their article on how Tracy developed and the trajectory of its path of destruction will shed more clarity with factual detail.

The catastrophic natural event that overwhelmed Darwin and killed 65 people began life on December 20, in 1974, in the cyclone breeding ground of the Arafura Sea, between Timor and West New Guinea. Starting as a tropical low-pressure system, it moved south and intensified. On 21st December, satellite photographs indicated that the system had become a tropical cyclone. At 10pm on 21st December the Tropical Cyclone Warning Centre at Darwin named the cyclone "Tracy" and issued the first warning to coastal communities between Goulburn and Bathurst Islands. The cyclone was then 200km north-northeast of Cape Don. By midnight on 23rd December, it was clear that Tracy was moving southwards. At 3am on 24th December, the cyclone rounded Cape Fourcray, on the southwest tip of Bathurst Island. Winds had increased to 120km/h. At noon on 24th December, forecasters noted that the cyclone had changed to a southeasterly course and was headed towards Darwin. A top priority warning was issued at 12.30pm on Christmas Eve: "Tracy is moving slowly closer to Darwin, very destructive winds of 120km/h with gusts at 150km/h are expected in the Darwin area tonight and tomorrow." The warning was widely broadcast, along with advice on the precautionary action individuals could take. It appears that as Tracy approached Darwin, the system may have narrowed and intensified. At 1am on Christmas Day the full force of the cyclone hit Darwin. Peak winds probably occurred soon after 3am, and may have reached velocities up to 250km/h. The centre of the cyclone system appears to have crossed the coast near Coconut Grove, then moved (approximately) along the main airport runway, then southeast away from Darwin. By noon on Christmas Day the system was near Fogg Dam and was degenerating into a rain depression.

Tracy sounded a death knell on the city, old Darwin was gone and a new city would need to rise like a phoenix out of the rubble and destruction. The official population of Darwin at the time was 45,000, however Darwin had a transient population so it may have been more, consequently there are at least 45,000 personal stories to tell about that night.

The official statistics of the event are as follows;

- Maximum wind speed was recorded at 217km/h before the anemometer ceased to function. It was estimated that subsequent wind gusts reached 250km/h.
- The storm surges recorded were 1.6m in Darwin harbour and estimated at 4m at Casuarina Beach.
- Rainfall was recorded at 255mm in 12 hrs.
- The death toll of 69 persons were 51 on land and 18 at sea.
- Injuries, 145 serious, 500 requiring medical treatment and thousands with minor injuries.
- Of twelve thousand homes, eight thousand were completely destroyed.

This year is the 50th anniversary of that terrifying event, I've buried the memory of it, could only refer to it in passing for fear of the horror of that night impacting my composure all over again. To speak of it still gives me cold shivers and can bring on a flood of tears. Ever since I've been fearful during thunder storms or strong winds which often precede rain events in the tropics, even in the desert and along our coastline. Often not going to bed if they occurred at night, sitting up fully dressed wearing sturdy footwear, having a torch handy in case disaster struck.

Perhaps it's now time for me to tell our story;

We heeded the warnings, had an emergency water supply, a torch at the ready, stored all loose outdoor items and taped the windows, that afternoon the sky looked ominous but like so many people in Darwin we were optimistic that the storm would miss us and all would be well. We put the children to bed then decorated our tree ready for Christmas. It was raining heavily and we could hear the wind howling in fury, the air pressure was dropping rapidly. Just before midnight a huge crash resounded as the roof from the house across the street hit the front of our house, hitting our living room and the children's bedroom, fortunately we had put them into the guest room, using their bedding Mick had prepared an area down by the bathroom with mattresses and pillows where we had been advised to shelter during the storm. An SES worker hammered on our door to check that we were okay, Mick could barely hold the door against the wind. I truly hope to this day this man and his team made it to a safe place.

We moved the children out of their beds to the 'shelter area' and sat in the dark listening to our small transistor radio for updates, the power had long gone off, then the radio went dead. The noise level of the wind was deafening, our ears started to really feel the pressure. Then we lost our roof, the sound of it tearing away was indescribable, now we could see lightning flashes through the gaps in our ceiling panels which were spreading and bouncing, the rain driving in through the gaps, Mick said we had to get out of the house before it broke up, he'd long voiced his concern that the tilt panel construction was virtually a 'house of cards' and wished that we had chosen a conventional build, we were waiting for the eye to pass over so that we could make our escape, the noise and wind suddenly abated, Mick tried the back door, he could open it now, then a tremendous crash sounded.

Mick shone the torch down our staircase to check if our way was clear, the hand rail of our back stairs was almost flattened, there was just room for us to get down in single file. He went first with the torch, radio and Brenton, I had Paul by the arm on the leeward side protecting him with my body should there be another gust and our cat in a pillowcase tucked under my other arm. We made it into our ground level storeroom, as we shut the door the storm started to rage again with what felt like increased fury. Mick built a shelter over the children with solid items we had stored, we sat in waist deep water, the pool had overflowed and filled the storeroom. We prayed that at least the children would survive under the makeshift shelter if the building above should collapse. We sat in darkness watching the lightning flashes through what were supposed to be solid walls. Then towards morning the cat sat up and started to groom herself, the pressure in our ears eased, it was over. By the grace of God, we had all survived. The boys didn't complain once, listened to what we were telling them, we tried our best to be reassuring. It had been a long night, I think I must have been in shock; I was so cold and shivering to the point that my teeth were chattering, functioning on autopilot.

* * *

The Power of Nature

It was still raining when Mick opened the door, sheets of roofing iron were floating on the wind, there was devastation as far as we could see. We really couldn't take it in yet, it seemed so surreal. Our car parked under the house was saved by the neighbour's roof, it was a dry place to put the children. We had picnic blankets to wrap around them, they were safe now. The cat settled on the rear window ledge. Gradually people started to emerge from the wreckage. Our neighbour to the left had one room left standing, the toilet, he and his wife and two children had sheltered in there all night. The house to the right had a couple of walls still standing as did ours, our ceiling panels had served to demolish our neighbours house as they blew out. A fire extinguisher punched a hole clean through the concrete panel front wall of the house 2 doors down. To our right, two doors down nothing was left, the floor boards in our pool were from that house.

That must have been the dreadful crash we heard just before we made our escape down the stairs, the family living there had become friends, we knew them well, they had introduced our boys to the pleasure of chewing on a stalk of sugar cane and the exotic taste of salted plums. We had spent many pleasant afternoons with them. Our house of cards had fallen down, but had provided us more shelter than the conventional built house of our friends.

Mick went out to check on the family. He brought their two little girls to me, both injured, one with an obviously broken leg, the other with a deep open wound on her little forehead. She was just a baby, perhaps eight months old, they were both freezing cold and in shock from exposure, the baby could barely whimper, the other little one, aged about two years was so traumatised she didn't make a sound, just looked at me with her big brown eyes. I wrote their names on their arms in Texta, which I found in the glove box, concerned that in the chaos they would be separated and not identified. I wrapped each one in a blanket and placed them together on the front seat of the car. Then so that I could go and assist Mick, gave one of the little girls to each of our sons to hold, shared body warmth the best way to warm the girls.

Worse was to come, Mick found their parents, all of them had been blown out when the house blew apart. They were lying in the driving rain and mud, Jannine was alive but couldn't move, Mick covered her with a tarpaulin, (his swag cover) to shelter her from the rain and told her the children were safe. Then a neighbour helped him put Frank onto a door and they carried him to shelter, he died a short time later.

The man helping Mick was an ex-army SAS soldier, he broke down; saying he thought that he wouldn't have to deal with death and destruction anymore, fortunately his wife and adult sons were unharmed, although their home was gone, just a pile of rubble, his roof wrapped around the piers of our house.

Mick's walk to the police station at Casuarina was treacherous, the roads impassable due to the debris. He walked there to report the fate of our neighbours, finding the duty police in a wrecked building still doing their jobs, not knowing the fate of their own families. The only communication now was two-way radio, calls went out and earth-moving equipment was mobilised to clear roads. We managed to get the shattered family to safety and medical attention. Mick was shaking when he returned, having put the body of our neighbour into the makeshift mortuary hurt him deeply and what else he saw that day shocked him badly.

We felt so lucky that we had survived unharmed, we had a dry place for our children in the car and our trusty swag. Later that day Mick ventured back upstairs to survey what was left, when he came back down, he handed me a small sodden package; it was to have been my Christmas gift, I opened it to find a small wrist watch, the face cloudy with moisture. He looked over my shoulder and said "perhaps it will go when it dries out". It did, it doesn't anymore but I have treasured it ever since.

The speed with which everyone pulled together and started to organise and make sense of the situation was nothing short of amazing. We had so much food and no refrigeration, by evening there was almost a street party atmosphere and we shared what we had, huddled together, everyone telling tales of their survival. Disasters bring out the best and the worst in people as we know. One neighbour took the tarpaulin sheltering Jannine while Mick was getting her to medical assistance. Mick reclaimed it so that we could make up our swag for the night. Our city was destined to survive, the spirit of the people was in shock but not broken, the phoenix would once again rise.

Mick's parents arrived in Darwin once the highway was cleared, seemingly not to assist us but to wail because we hadn't turned up for Christmas Lunch. Audrey's (my mother in-law) priority left me quite stunned; she began complaining that the power was still out and Batchelor was being run on an emergency generator, but only for a few hours at night. I can only assume it was shock, she had been in London during WWII and had memories of that time. Leonard, (my father in-law) had come out of retirement and started working again, at an architectural firm in Darwin, so understandably wanted to check on colleagues. Audrey agreed that Mick and I could bring the children down to Batchelor while we sorted things out. That arrangement lasted one night!

Next morning Mick went out early to find Dan the town manager and ask about accommodation, Dan told him of a 2-bedroom house where a couple of single men had been living, they were away interstate. No-one was sure if they would be back given the current circumstances so we could have the house initially short-term. While I was getting ready the smell of toast led the children down to the kitchen, I heard Audrey ask the children what they wanted, when they replied 'breakfast' she told them to get their lazy mother to tend to their needs. I certainly complied; without a word we left the house. There was an emergency shelter set up at the local sporting club in Batchelor and meals were available at the canteen for cyclone refugees, so that was where we went, later Mick met us there with his good news. We officially became squatters. I packed up all personal belongings left in the house by the previous occupants, (including an envelope containing a considerable amount of money which I found taped to the inside of the refrigerator,) listing everything and all was placed into safe storage at the local police station. This is how we found ourselves just 2 doors down from where we had been living just a few short years previously.

In February Brenton started school and Paul kindergarten. We'd attempted to salvage some of our belongings, without much luck. Everything soft, clothing, linen, etc. was rotting and unsalvageable, covered in glass; the furniture similarly ruined. Mick was able to rescue his rifles, they were safely buried under a pile of debris and after a good clean and oiling were as good as new, he even found his government issued .303 rifle which saved a lot of red tape. His pistol was safely locked away in our possession. The few items we did pack up were looted while we were down at the emergency centre getting food for our family. As I said the best and the worst.

The insurance assessors arrived in Darwin, we were told by one of them that we had indeed been living in a house of cards, some of the ceiling panels hadn't been bolted down, the bolts hadn't lined up with the holes so had been cut off to make the panels fit. Concrete panels sitting in grooves in the pillars were maybe ok vertically, but horizontally there was nothing holding the ceiling down, just its own weight. He wasn't prepared to give us a copy of his written report. Darwin was one of the fastest growing places in Australia at the time, there had been an acute housing shortage, perhaps the building code was inadequate, maybe there were modifications made to plans to get houses built, houses were springing up like mushrooms, we will never know. Nothing could have prevented the disaster of Cyclone Tracy "the power of nature".

Mick met with the people at the reconstruction commission. Navy personnel came and cleared the debris out of our disaster zone. They were cheerful and considerate; I was present as they sorted through the remnants of our possessions and asked me whenever they found something salvageable whether it was to keep or not. We did salvage the camphor wood chest containing a lot of the wedding presents we never used but kept because of the memories they held. When the cleanup crew left Mick found me sitting in the middle of what had once been our home crying over a broken gift from my sister; he put his arm around me and said 'look at the bright side', with the insurance payout we'll be debt free. Always the optimist he sometimes came out with the strangest things at the oddest times. He then confessed that he hadn't liked being tied to a place by a mortgage.

The heavy machinery moved in and removed the remaining concrete panels, we now had what became known as a 'dancefloor' with stairs leading up to what had once been the floor of our house. We salvaged a bunch of bananas that we'd hung to ripen before the storm and shared them with our neighbours in Batchelor. Darwin was fast becoming a ghost town, with people being evacuated. I had refused to go, inwardly knowing that it would be difficult to get back, not prepared to separate the family. The children had had enough trauma for such young lives just getting through this, Paul had started sleepwalking, Brenton didn't say much, went off to school, played with the other children and his brother.

The insurance payout went through and we had enough to pay out the residual mortgage. We now owned the land and remaining improvements, not quite back to square one, we had the option of selling or one day rebuilding. We stayed at Batchelor our tenancy now official. Friends had a caravan and were looking for a place to park, they approached us and asked what our plans were regarding the property, we felt fortunate to have something left and agreed that they could use the site, we had a temporary power pole connected, cleaned the pool and repaired the pump, modified the downstairs laundry, installing a toilet and shower so they could use it as a bathroom as well as laundry.

Miraculously the garden began to recover, they enclosed the under-croft for privacy and extra living space, the front stairs leading up to the 'dancefloor' were still there years later when we went back to Darwin for a visit. They made it their home. Eventually the NT Administration bought the block. We were paid the pre-cyclone land value and an amount for the improvements, our pool and remaining concrete slab and driveway.

Darwin received a lot of help from friends and strangers after the cyclone, the generosity of the Australian people in times of natural disasters is well documented. Neighbouring countries were also sending aid. We received the sum of $200 as a re-establishment grant, Mick came home with 2 shining red bicycles for our little boys, a belated Christmas present. Mother and aunt put together a collection of household items and linen which was gratefully received. A local family gave us school uniforms for Brenton and clothes for both the children, we'd lost everything of theirs as their bedroom was shattered.

We were able to salvage a couple of Paul's totems, the coolamon was broken, he still has the ceremonial spear and stone axe head; the boomerang disappeared. I like to think that the spirit meaning behind them had put a protective aura over our young son and thank Whitefoot for his blessing. In the days immediately following the storm Mick had been assisting the department vets with euthanizing the injured and abandoned animals, he said there were so many, it took a dreadful emotional toll. No one who was in Darwin during the cyclone or the immediate aftermath escaped without trauma.

In May 1975 we went to Tasmania for a family holiday, the boys got to play in snow on Mt Wellington, we visited Barbara who was living in Melbourne at the time on the way, she told the boys that she had a boa constrictor living behind the 'fridge, this intrigued them greatly. It was another year of disaster for Australia, a bulk carrier collided with the Tasman Bridge, two piers collapsed along with 127metres of bridge decking. Four cars ran over the gap and plunged into the Derwent River, twelve people lost their lives in the disaster, seven crew members on the ship and five motorists.

Mick had been stationed at Menling Abattoir again as the city needed fresh meat and Darwin Abattoir was still closed. Soon after the dry was here again, and the bush trips started all over again. The cycle was repeating, entering the next phase and reconstruction began. We had now acquired a little dog; Mick found her walking along the highway on one of his trips to Darwin. She happily jumped into the vehicle with him, she was wearing a collar with the name 'Candy' on it and was blind in one eye. So many dogs and cats, domestic pets of all sorts and some livestock had become victims of Cyclone Tracy, it was heartbreaking.

It was time to re-group and decide where we'd like our future to take us. Were we content to continue and start again in Darwin or even Alice Springs? The Department had so far not considered posting Mick there. Mick sent letters of inquiry to Tasmanian, Victorian and South Australian Agricultural Departments; they were answered sympathetically but there were no vacancies that year. We were also concerned for the future education of our boys; it was customary to send children away to boarding school for higher education either into Queensland or South Australia. Neither of us wanted to hand our sons to someone else during these most formative years. Darwin had a high school but there was no guarantee we would be in Darwin; we could easily be transferred to another bush station like Elliott.

We started to scour newspaper advertisements looking for options and housing affordability. We had been living frugally and with the sale of our land had savings. A place in WA looked appealing, I knew and liked the area, Beaconsfield was the suburb adjacent to South Fremantle. Mother did the inspection, gave it the thumbs up, the bank did a valuation, again a positive. We bought the place sight unseen. Mick tendered his resignation. The school year had finished and the wet season was upon us again. We packed up our meagre belongings, loaded everything onto State Shipping, including the car, booked our tickets and together with the dog and cat boarded a plane for Western Australia, the future would take care of itself one way or another, we were optimistic as always and had a PLAN.

My parents had formally separated now, father was living in Sydney with his new wife. Mother at the family home in Hamilton Hill, she had a new job and was travelling, enjoying her new found freedom. She seemed happier than she had for a lot of years and she had a nice male friend. It was really the first time I was estranged from father, not my choice but circumstance. We still corresponded but he had changed. His new wife and stepsons occupied him now. He also changed jobs again, was now working on phosphate carriers. My sister was still living in Melbourne and flying crisscross around Australia. Mick and I together with our sons were starting over, ready to embrace yet another change. We arrived in early February, late evening, there was a scorching hot wind howling and there was talk of the plane being diverted to Kalgoorlie; but we eventually landed in Perth. Collected our luggage and pets from the quarantine hanger, dog Candy now on a leash and Puss-cat in the dog carrier. Her carrier had been confiscated; they didn't allow fruit boxes with cats inside past the quarantine point. The cat must have created the problem, I believe that tropical fruit regularly came into the State from the Northern Territory.

- The last decade had started with our Prime Minister and his government being sacked by our Governor General.
- A city left in ruins due to the devastation of Cyclone Tracy tearing the city apart and wrecking many lives, shattering hopes and dreams in the process.
- Our troops were finally home from Vietnam, more broken lives, eighteen was the new voting age and eighteen-year-olds were officially allowed to have a beer.
- Darwin was on the road to recovery thanks to the efforts of so many. It would be a long road, but every journey starts with a first step, that step was taken on the morning after the cyclone when with open eyes we faced the devastation and ruin, turned to our neighbours and reached out a helping hand.
- Darwin had a long relationship with Timor, this had significant impact beginning in 1975 when Indonesia invaded the former Portuguese territory of East Timor following the 'Carnation Revolution' in Portugal. After the revolution Portugal divested itself of its former colonies, leaving the majority of them without a clear plan for the future and self-rule, leading to turbulent times in those colonies.
- From Cyclone Tracy to the Bali bombings, the tropical city of Darwin has on numerous occasions become an epicentre of major inter-national events one of those was the humanitarian crisis that followed East Timor's independence vote in 1999.

5

Western Australia - A Fresh Start

Beaconsfield

The house at Beaconsfield was quirky, originally a 2-bedroom cottage with an under-croft garage, verandahs at the front and down one sides and at the rear. The verandahs had been enclosed into 2 sleepouts and a back porch, which was a shame as the rear of the property had the most amazing views to the ocean. The original second bedroom had become a vestibule or study from which there was entry to a granny flat and one of the sleepouts. The granny flat was currently let, the tenants having use of the garage, it also had a street entrance. The garden was well established with lawn and roses at the front, the back yard had been divided into 2 sections, the one nearest the house was fully paved except for a small section of grass to one side under the clothes line. In the centre of the courtyard was an enormous fishpond and rock garden, goldfish were resident in the pond. We had purchased the house from a second-hand furniture dealer, knowing of our recent plight he left the house fully furnished with some quite nice furniture. It was a solid start for whatever came next.

When we had settled and the children were enrolled at school, Mick and I set about trying to find a viable small business. In the meantime, mother's friend Josef, who owned a butcher's shop and made continental small-goods, employed Mick on a casual basis. He was keen to take him on full-time, Mick was concerned that it wouldn't work out long term and could lead to conflict, so declined the offer. Some years later Josef offered Brenton an apprenticeship should he be interested in the trade.

We engaged a broker, looked at many options, even some country hotels, eventually settling on a lawn mowing business. It came complete with vehicle, plant and equipment and a full book of clients. The accounts we were shown looked to provide reasonable takings, we planned to expand the southern client base and sell the goodwill of the northern clients as the business grew, eventually expanding into garden maintenance. Too good to be true! I'm hearing echoes. Naturally there is always a downside

In the first month we discovered there was a cash-flow problem, people didn't pay their bills on time, those in the more affluent areas were the worst, a small business of this nature can't carry creditors. With 75% of the clients based north of the Swan River, (we were living on south side) there was way too much travel, the rates weren't right, set way too low, not even covering overheads. We wrote to all the clients advising that we needed to increase the rates, we lost a number of those that did pay, those on pensions or living hand to mouth, saying they couldn't afford any increase. We learnt that goodwill is worth very little, wasn't a tangible asset

Additionally human nature being what it is, some clients couldn't be satisfied, complaining they could see lines from the mower, wanting the direction of the cut reversed, which wasn't always possible due to the orientation of the property, some wanted the clippings removed, some not, evening phone calls of complaints were an occurrence I didn't like to handle. There were safety issues as well, hurdles like retaining walls to manoeuvre the mower up and over, the client insisting on the heavy reel mower to be used, not the rotary. One misadventure resulted when the reel mower escaped, Mick said he had to lean it back so that it could cut the grass under a tree, he lost his hold and somehow the throttle jammed, the mower escaped careering down the slope and eventually came to rest against the shed, in the process shattering a sheet of cladding, oops! Some of the ladies were lonely and seeking company, wanting Mick to stay and have a cuppa with them. The men wanted to chat, but he had more lawns to cut and didn't have time. Others used the opportunity to fill his trailer with garden waste, not a nice thing to do. He told one client that he wasn't coming back due to the unpaid bill, when she asked what else she could do, he told her to buy a goat. Once he got paid with a pair of ducks. Nice birds but we couldn't barter with them. I tried working with him when the children were at school, this meant running 2 vehicles so wasn't the solution to getting more done in a day, just increased the overheads. This venture didn't live up to expectations. We broke up the round, sold off the clients and plant to other operators, traded the vehicle on a Ute for Mick. We recouped some of our investment but funds were starting to run low.

Mick registered for unemployment benefits, it really galled him, we kept scouring the situations vacant column in the papers, the bit of rent we were getting for the flat helped. Mick applied for lots of positions but wasn't trained for city life. We spent some days on the public golf course using mother's clubs. Mick heard that if he lined up early in the morning at the gate of the meat exporter at Robb's Jetty with the other men, some of them would get chosen for a day's work. If they were busy, this could sometimes lead to permanent casual work. He presented at the lineup next day, was chosen and issued with 'Eskimo clothing' to start work in the chillers, loading out carcasses and boxed meat on conveyor belts to be loaded into trucks. The carcasses had to be taken off the hanging rail and placed onto the conveyor, hard physical work. Still, he presented again daily for a week, they picked him every day. The following week he was on the permanent casual payroll. Things went smoothly until he got the 'flu which turned into pneumonia and he missed work for three days due to being bedbound. We'd let them know what had happened but there wasn't a job when he recovered.

I could see he was losing heart so one day when Mick was doing a delivery for Josef, I rang the Department of Agriculture in South Perth, managed to speak to the right person and found out that they were recruiting for a couple of positions, one was a Ranger position at Halls Creek, the other a Stock Inspector at Midland Sale Yards. We had 24 hours to get the applications in before they closed. I'd never typed so fast in my life, Mick hand delivered them, we made the deadline. He was granted interviews for both positions and got offered both jobs. Would we be going north again or staying this time? Together we considered what would be our best option, what would be best for the boys, they needed some stability surely. Halls Creek meant feral animal control, herds of wild donkeys were a particular problem, the other, Noogoora Burr. Eradication programmes meant using toxic herbicides. Flying in 'choppers shooting donkeys was just too unpalatable, regardless of pest status Mick loved donkeys and wouldn't be able to bring himself to shoot them. Besides, boarding school for the boys would be a reality, the very reason we had left the Territory. The salary was higher than the Stock Inspector's position. Irrespective of tax breaks and zone allowances, the Stock Inspector's position won out. Mick commenced work at the Midland Sale Yards, it was familiar work as Mick had worked at the Gepps Cross Saleyards in Adelaide for a time drafting sheep. This was different as he would be checking for lice and foot-rot.

***

Serpentine

Midland was a fair distance to travel from Beaconsfield so we started to look for a home closer, settled on a place on acreage at Serpentine. During the school break we moved, hadn't had any trouble selling our place, it was snapped up. The Serpentine house had been transported to a vacant 10-acre lot. A farm had been subdivided and we had the lot closest to the Reserve, it was nice to be near the bush again. Although it was undeveloped, we felt we could turn the place into somewhere nice and it had a Kennel Licence so there was scope to develop a business later on. We now had a small mortgage. The boys were enrolled into Serpentine Primary School for term 3. Pusscat soon claimed her territory and settled in. We had brought with us 2 ferrets who had joined us as well as the 2 ducks. Fortunately, one of the kennels served very well as a poultry house. The previous owner had left us some chickens. It was a straight run up the highway for Mick to get to work at Midland.

Our little rescue dog was a strange little creature, when we were living at Beaconsfield, she would regularly take herself down to the shopping centre opposite the primary school and wait on the pavement outside one of the shops until I got a call to come and collect her. The boys usually walked to and from school so she must have been following them without my seeing her. She started doing the same at Serpentine, although I was taking them to school in the car and picking them up at the end of the day. I would collect the children, the mail and pickup any necessities from the general store and the dog. It didn't take long for people to know she was ours and what the routine was. One day though she wasn't at home or in town, she'd disappeared. We can only assume she'd been walking along the highway and got picked up, just as she had come to us in Batchelor after the cyclone. I searched the verges and roadsides for days but found no trace of her, so that was what we chose to believe.

That summer there was a fire up in the hills, Mick and I joined in to fight the fire before we all got burnt out, we lost the grass in the top paddock but the house paddock was saved. It looked awful afterwards, all black and burnt, all the way up the hill to the lookout. The worst thing about the fire was the little animals in the bush trying to escape the flames, with their fur scorched. Nature can be very cruel.

The boys met their maternal grandfather for the first time that year. His shipped docked at Kwinana to unload phosphate and was in port for a couple of days, we drove down to meet him. It was good to see him but he'd definitely changed, spoke of things I wasn't familiar with. He showed us the engine room, the heart of the ship, so much of it was now computerised and he hadn't kept up with technology, he was now ranked number four, when once he'd been First ship's Engineer, and people half his age were in charge. I got the impression he wasn't happy; he began to talk of retiring.

Barbara, still living in Melbourne, suffered a dreadful accident, she was hit by a truck while crossing the street, was badly injured, mother flew over to be by her side. I prayed she would be alright; I couldn't contemplate a world without her in it. After a long stay in hospital, she was finally allowed to come home to Western Australia. She was as weak as a kitten and had lost so much weight. Her flying career was over, although she did try to resume it, she too had to start over, turn a page and write the next chapter. She chose to go back to university; graduated with distinction having completed her studies, a qualified social worker. A new career path opened to her.

A sign on the roadside advertising geese for sale drew my attention, thinking about Christmas I turned in to buy a goose, remembering that goose was a particular luxury back in Europe and hoping to surprise mother. Only this one was a live goose; he joined our chickens and ducks out in the house paddock. Mick had also adopted a German Shepherd; we called her Heidi. Mick later added a couple of sheep to the menagerie, someone had to eat the grass. There was a water supply issue which wasn't ideal, the only supply line was to the adjoining dairy farm, we and our other neighbour were reliant on their water. Subsidiary lines had been put in place; however, the pressure was minimal, especially when the dairy was operating. Mick put in a water tank which filled when there was water available and connected a pressure pump feeding into the house to solve the issue.

What came next? Don't plan too far ahead is something I'd learnt by now. Mick was transferred to Bunbury, it was early November, he had to start immediately, the Stock Inspector in Bunbury was retiring at the end of the year and he had to be there for the handover. Mick was installed in a flat and started the weekly commute. Really not what we needed or had hoped for. Over the next couple of months, he managed to find a farm house for us to rent at Dardanup, we would be able to move in time for the new school year. We now had the issue of paying rent and a mortgage, renting our place out wasn't a good option so we put it up for sale, it sat on the market without much interest, seems hobby farms weren't that popular yet. Mick went to see the bank and negotiated with them so that we could suspend our mortgage payments and settle when the sale was finalised.

* * *

Dardanup

At the end of the school year we packed up once again and moved into the farm-house at Dardanup, taking the menagerie with us, and just enough furniture to suit the 2-bedroom cottage with sleepouts. There were grape vines trailing along the back verandah, in the evening we could see rats running along the rafters and feeding on the bunches of grapes, there was also a fat brush-tail possum living in the wall cavity of the out-house. He liked grapes also. The house was dubbed the 'mouse house'. The children were enrolled at the Dardanup Primary School for the start of the year. We made regular trips back to check on the house at Serpentine, after one 'home open' showing we found it was stripped bare. Curtains, furniture, the water tank and pump, even the new gates we'd put up, it was a blow. It took eight months to sell, the remaining attraction was the Kennel Licence. A dog breeder purchased it to establish kennels. We were debt free again, had paid a bit more interest but were left with enough for a house in Bunbury and a decent car for Mick.

My father died while we were living at Dardanup, tragically one stormy night in Esperance he came to grief. I received the letter he'd posted to me that night about a week later. The first phone call we got was to tell us he was missing, asking if we'd heard from him. I told them no, he'd been to visit us just a short time earlier when the ship had docked at Kwinana and Mick had gone to get him for an overnight visit, we'd arranged for him to come again next time they were in port. He wasn't found for two days, then we got the sad news that he was gone from us. We were told that he must have slipped coming back on board. Barbara and mother were both in shock as you can imagine. We were all numb, our emotions in turmoil.

What happened next would film like a black comedy. The ship's owners had been instructed by the new Mrs H, his second wife, that he was to be cremated in Esperance and his ashes scattered at sea. When Mick heard this and saw the look on my face he put an alternative arrangement in place. He arranged to have our father's body brought to Fremantle, then told the shipping company they were still welcome to pay for the funeral and do as Mrs H had instructed but it would be happening in Fremantle so that his family could say goodbye. The shipping company sent a representative to the funeral. We got to say goodbye to our father and mother to the man she was married to for 25 years. She never referred to herself as a divorcee, she was his widow. I received a nasty letter from Mrs H's parents later, which I had much joy setting fire to and never answered. Mrs H sent a letter of condolence together with a copy of fathers will, my sister had met her and said she seemed a decent person.

Losing father was the first time I had to deal with the emotions of a grief far greater than any I had ever experienced. Losing my pets was terrible, it was sad and very unfair that they should be taken away from me, that little creatures who had made me so happy and loved unconditionally had such short lives. I had real trouble reconciling his death. I was sad he was gone, yet so very angry, we had finally reconnected, there were gaps in the years where our lives had taken us down different paths, he had only just met his grandsons at the ages where they could have bonded. I had so much I wanted to share with him but underlying all of it was the fact that I wanted him to let me know that I had won his approval. I had never felt that I pleased him enough or made him proud of me, there always seemed to be a feeling that he placed conditions on how our relationship stood, he was volatile if things didn't go to plan or his expectations weren't met, now that chance was gone forever.

I was angry that on the single occasion he could have got to know his grandchildren, he scarcely acknowledged them, spent hours sitting on our back verandah telling us how wonderful his new wife was and regaling stories about his step sons. Apparently not interested in us at all, not asking how we had managed after Cyclone Tracy. So self-absorbed, oblivious of the celebratory dinner I had prepared, not even bothering to come to the table to eat. The dinner was ruined, keeping it warm rendered it inedible, long after the children had gone to bed he finally came in and patted me on the head as if I was a dog and told me not to worry about it. Didn't even ask what I had prepared, the beautiful bird had given up his life for no reason, it was the goose I had purchased when we were living at Serpentine, it grieved me deeply, I wasn't squeamish about eating meat as long as the animal had the best life possible and was going to feed the family and all parts would be utilised, but I abhorred waste and needless sacrifice.

I felt that so much more than my father's physical being had been taken, I now also knew that when he divorced my mother, he had shed me and my sister as well. We no longer mattered to him. I told Mick how I felt and he assured me that I was all he'd ever wanted and had nothing to prove. Being with Mick gave me the confidence to face the world and have belief in my ability to conquer life's challenges.

Apart from losing father tragically I had enjoyed living in the 'mouse house'. The little town and community had made us feel welcome, the neighbours were generous and friendly. A fluffy white kitten joined our menagerie, the boys named him 'Yarloop', the name written on the box he'd travelled in. The garden was flourishing after I tidied it up, there were some lovely old established plants around the house, camelias, hydrangeas and other shrubs, bulbs came up en-mass, we had permission to pick fruit from the family orchard. A share-farmer grew crops down by the creek, potatoes in winter and pumpkins in summer, we were welcome to take what we needed of those. We got fresh milk from the dairy daily. I travelled around to all the farms and cattle sales with Mick and got to know the district. Mick was home most evenings as he was working locally. Attending sales, doing Port quarantine for the live sheep export trade, beef cattle carcass classification at the meat-works.

I believed the boys were happy and doing okay, they purposely missed the school bus most morning so I had to take them to school. They got invited to birthday parties, Brenton started to play in the school hockey team, they swam in the irrigation channels to cool off. There was lots of room for them to be 'boys', riding their bikes and roaming about on the farm. Was I getting soft, needing a permanent nest for my family to settle in? I knew we had to move again as our landlord was due back at the end of the year and needed the house for himself. Through a friendly estate agent, we purchased a house by the beach in Bunbury and packed up once again. He said he'd stay in touch, introduce us to his mates at the Bunbury Football Club and invite us to his home to meet his family.

So ended 1977.

* * *

Raising a family

It seemed just a short time ago that I felt young, carefree, full of dreams. Have life's events and uncertainties changed me? Do my responsibilities weigh too heavily, have I lost my joy, forgotten how to laugh? My expectations dulled, yet I'm still unsure of myself, second guessing almost every move. Once I was full of bravado and a decent dose of confidence. Is that what happens as you get older and mature? I was never trained or prepared for parenthood or being responsible for other lives, to guide them into the world.

I came across this verse a long time ago and have kept a copy of it for inspiration and as a reminder that having a family comes with personal challenge. Facing the challenge of parenting isn't easy, the best I could do was to stay true to my principles and teach them the only way I knew how.

> *Challenge*
> *How shall we teach a Child to reach*
> *Beyond himself and touch the stars*
> *We who have stooped so much?*
> *How shall we say to him,*
> *'The way of life is through the gate of love'*
> *We who have learnt to hate?*
> *How shall we tell a child to dwell*
> *With honour, live and die for truth,*
> *We who have lived a lie?*
> *How shall we dare to teach him prayer*
> *And turn him toward the way of faith,*
> *We who no longer pray?*
>   *Mildred Howland*

Have I measured up; how could I know? Their arrival into my life was an amazing experience and I shall carry the memory of every one of the days we shared forever. I'd not been a parent before so I had to learn hour by hour, day by day, with Mick by my side. I am very proud of the men they are today.

I hope I was able to give enough; my choice was to be a fulltime parent, (not work outside the home) until I felt sure they would be alright. My early employment was school hours, this still gave me time for their after-school activities, sports training, or the beach on summer afternoons. I tried to take an interest in and know their friends and the people they associated with, always concerned for their safety and wellbeing without stifling their curiosity, creativity or sense of adventure. Prepared healthy food for them to grow healthy bodies and they did with relatively few problems, barring accidents brought on by the rough and tumble nature of being boys. Was it enough? I hope it was.

* * *

Bunbury

We'd settled on an older home near the beach, a lovely bungalow with two sets of leadlight French doors, opening onto the front verandah and bay windows in the living room and main bedroom. You could hear the surf breaking on the rocks at night. The surf club and swimming beach a short walk away. A sport and recreation ground opposite and a lighthouse on the hill. The boys were enrolled at school, (this made 7 schools in 5 years for Brenton) understandably both nervous about being the new kids again. Paul's teacher told me that he walked in, looked around at the faces looking back at him and asked 'haven't you seen a new kid before?' which broke the ice. Brenton's teacher told me he would reassure Brenton, let him know that it was his first day at this school too. Our estate agent was true to his word and introduced us at the Bunbury Football Club, at Friday night drinks where we got to know a few people and formed a social network. Once we had settled and the summer was over, I was keen to rejoin the workforce and augment the family income.

I tried working in real estate, was hired on a retainer to do listings, attained my sales representative's licence and sold a couple of properties, but being new to town made it a difficult job as I didn't have the local knowledge and contacts. Next, I got a job at an insurance company, I'd applied for an admin position but the manager thought I'd be good at sales. I did the initial training, attended seminars and gave it my best effort, I was assigned to Collie, where I knew no-one, I started to cold call on people and introduce myself. I made quite a few sales but it was hard with travel and my natural reserve, cold calling was taking an emotional toll. Cyclone Albie travelled down the West coast and caused quite a lot of damage in Bunbury, we lost our front porch and two chimneys, the sand-blasting from the beach-sand literally blew the paint off the weatherboards on the western side of the house. Being caught in Collie, with trees falling across the roads on the way home, a very concerned husband and wide-eyed children greeting me on arrival, sealed the decision to end my career in sales. We repaired the damage to the house, did some internal renovations and put in a vegetable garden.

Mick was still working around Bunbury but was also called on to go further afield as the 'foot rot' and 'lice' eradication programmes had commenced. This meant nights away, although not for as long as in the Territory. He was away for an extended period when he was sent north to the Kimberly region for coastal surveillance. Indonesian fishermen were coming into Australian waters fishing for Trochus shell and the risk for introducing exotic diseases into Australia was deemed high as the boats sometimes had monkeys aboard, Trochus was a prized commodity used to make buttons. The patrol boat he was on captured two vessels which were impounded, the crews being sent back to Java. One of the vessels was exhibited at the Fremantle Maritime Museum for a time, the other was burnt. Mick marvelled at the construction of these vessels saying they were a work of art, examples of skilled craftsmanship. He told us usual practice if the boats hadn't landed was for them to be boarded, most of their ration of rice poured into the sea, then they were warned to turn around and sail back to their homeland. If they made landfall they were impounded, the crews interred before being repatriated.

I recently listened to an interview on ABC radio which was about trade and interaction between Australia and Asia predating European settlement. This story made me curious to learn more, given that I knew of the Indonesian fishermen's history of sailing to the Kimberly coast for Trochus. I found some interesting information;

Matthew Flinders noted his encounter with Makassar people in his journal in 1803. The article I read states the following: From about 1700, hundreds of fishermen sailed each year from Makassar on the island of Sulawesi (Indonesia) to the Arnhem Land coast to an area they called Marege. Makasar traded with Aboriginal people, harvesting and processing trepang (sea cucumber) for their trade with China. The Makasar did not settle in Arnhem Land but did have an influence on the Indigenous people's society and ritual.

After Federation the Australian Government banned trepangers from Makassar in order to protect Australia's 'territorial integrity' and to encourage a local trepang industry. In 1907 the last prau (boat) from Makassar visited Arnhem Land. [2]

---

[2] Information from the National Museum – Australia. Defining Moments: Trade with the Makasar

After the event of Cyclone Albie, I started to look for alternative employment. I turned down a job at the local TV station in the film library cuing commercials as the hours didn't suit our family dynamic, the job required a 6am start. Mick had to start early most mornings so I needed to be home to get the children ready for school.

Eventually I was successful in gaining a position at the local veterinary clinic, it was perfect as it was school hours, although like with every job there were some negatives, I was bitten by a dog, he was very frightened of the strange smells in the clinic, I had to take him to his kennel as the nurses were busy with other tasks. In the process he snapped and bit my hand, the fright was worse than the bite. I loved working there, especially meeting the animals, and the people who brought them in excited about their new puppy or kitten or concerned for their ageing pet, the farmers who needed help for livestock concerned for the welfare of both their animals and livelihood. One lady could talk for hours about the pedigree of every cow in her herd, it was sometimes difficult to end a phone call with her. I think she must have been very lonely, her cows being her family. My duties were varied and covered all aspects of office management from reception to payroll and bookkeeping. I learnt a lot about animal health, nutrition, training, first aid and potential health issues by osmosis. Mother had done well sending me to Business College.

The boys were playing sports and had joined the surf club, spent a lot of time at the beach. It was a summer of sun and surf. Mick's parents had followed us to Western Australia and settled at Binningup Beach, they were at our house when Brenton broke his arm. He'd hit a rut where the bitumen had been badly repaired and the front wheel of his bicycle twisted, bucking him off. Rather than providing care and comfort his grandmother put a cotton-wool ball onto an open graze on his hip and told him to toughen up. When I came in from work, he told me his arm really hurt and I could see it had started to swell and was very red.

I took him to hospital where it was x-rayed and splinted. He had a 'greenstick fracture' of the wrist, fortunately the grandparents had left by the time we got back or family relations would have been shredded. It took a lot of soaking to get the cotton-wool out of his wound. What made it worse in my eyes was that the woman was a trained nursing sister.

Brenton coveted a new bicycle, a 10-speed racer, the old dragster having lost favour, unbeknown to him the new bike was on lay-by, we meant it for him for Christmas, he got it for his birthday instead. Paul had asked for a BMX bike and with a few modifications his bike soon fitted the bill. A mini motorbike became the shared Christmas present instead. They had a lot of fun riding on a friend's farm and in our garden, including riding through the house and out the back door without bothering to open it first. So much for letting them watch action movies. The dog thought it looked like fun and followed suit, it was a half screen door and she jumped through the screen with ease.

Our German shepherd 'Heidi' had a good life in our beachside home and regularly went out with Mick to visit the farms, just riding in the Ute. The neighbour's dog had a bad attitude and resented Heidi, tormenting her by barking and growling at her through the fence incessantly. One evening the two of them came face to face at the beach, Heidi broke free and the corgi was rather sick and sorry for a good week or more as a result. We lost Heidi to snakebite which was awful and missed her very much for a long time.

Our two cats were happy and healthy, good mousers, not popular when they caught the pet mice the boys happened to be playing with in the back room. Mice have a rather strong odour so the mouse house was kept in the garage on the workbench, Yarloop, the fluffy white cat, spent many hours sitting on top of the mouse house until his weight eventually dislodged the netting and the mice ran free, the mice some coloured some white proliferated and there were multicoloured mice running about in the shed up until we left. Who knows, they could still be running about in the neighbourhood. Our chickens kept the long grass at the back of our block under control, we enjoyed the bonus of fresh eggs. The rooster 'Toulouse' was a particularly fine bird. We also acquired another pair of ferrets, the ones we'd had previously no longer with us. They had been sable pole-cats, our new ones were a pair of goldens. Not too long later they numbered three. Guinea pigs were added to the menagerie also.

Living in town was convenient but there were a lot of temptations for a pack of boys exploring the alleys and backstreets, concerns for potential trouble loomed. We decided to look at places more on the fringe or rural. A farm at Noggerup looked appealing at first but after consideration was impractical for our stage of life. Our estate agent told us about a semi-rural property on the south side of Bunbury. It was new, brick and tile on 1 acre of land, mostly bush, just the ¼ acre the house sat on was cleared. It was a speculative build, the builder had got into financial difficulties and it was a mortgagee sale, so we got it at a very reasonable price, although we did once again have a mortgage. Our place sold almost immediately for a good price as the zoning was approved for redevelopment, 6 units could be built on the land.

The following year Brenton started high school; Paul remained at the same primary school until he too went to the high school. I would drop them at school before going to work and pick them up in the afternoon. Paul had started playing junior AFL football for the Bunbury Football Club 'The Bulldogs', I became a one-eyed supporter. He won awards at the end of each season, he was quite fearless on the field, going in hard which led to him getting a broken nose and several other injuries.

Brenton was playing softball. During the match warm-up ½ dozen balls were being thrown around, Brenton was hit in the face, knocked to the ground. The coach didn't blink an eye or check on him. I managed to get him into the car and took him to the emergency department of our local hospital, he had concussion and a broken nose, was admitted and had to stay two days. I made chocolate eclairs and took them in for him. It was the first and last time I made choux pastry successfully.

When I was growing up, I didn't think about much beyond my needs and wants, parental sacrifice never entered my head. I took everything coming my way for granted. It was only later when I had a family of my own that I put them first. Mick and my sons became my sole focus, I rarely thought about myself anymore, suddenly life seemed so serious. I was missing the freedom and adventure of living in the Northern Territory, missing the big open plains, the wide horizon and the open road, the endless canopy of blue sky. The easy friendships, town people are difficult to get to know and live such closed lives by comparison. Life had become repetitious, mundane and more than a little dull.

6

Gelorup - The Struggle Years

After relocating to Gelorup to our bush block we set about taming the scrub. Paul made it very clear he didn't like the move but soon discovered his mate from Bunbury wasn't living far away and his almost BMX bike wasn't too bad for a bit of scrub bashing. Besides his mate had a motor bike, lived on 5 acres and there were rows between the grape vines to ride around in.

Our ferret numbers had increased, the first litter produced one little doe, the second time around both females had big litters. The ferrets were a lot of fun, so playful and full of mischief, they loved playing in their bath. The boys dug a maze of tunnels for them to run in and we took them out rabbiting now and then. We didn't get many rabbits but the ferrets had a lot of fun and often came out covered in gore, so I guess they got to enjoy the rabbits. They were very good at escaping. Our neighbour phoned one morning and asked if we would come and collect our weasel as it was enjoying their dog's breakfast and their dog was rather upset. We sold all the young ones in pairs when they were mature, just kept the original pair.

Brenton was interested in medieval armoury, so Mick got him a makeshift forge and anvil, he made a suit of armour complete with shield and sword. He named him 'Sir Pent' and emblazoned the shield with a mythical snake-dragon. His workmanship was such that this piece has stood the test of time, 'Sir Pent' proudly stands in Brenton's house to this day. Brenton also became skilful at woodwork and produced some very nice pieces of furniture. Paul also made nice pieces while at high school; I still have a lamp he made for me.

The afternoon of Paul's graduation from primary school there was to be a concert with skits by the students. We were all ready to go, Brenton went down to feed the ferrets, he just stood very still, I immediately knew something was wrong, Mick went to him, his buck had died, curled up in his hutch as if asleep. Brenton was heartbroken, said he knew something was wrong before he opened the cage as the morning milk hadn't been touched. We buried him before we left for the end of year breakup. The little doe followed soon after. Little animals give so much joy in the short time they have on this earth. We got a pair of rabbits next. Risky as there was no vaccine against myxomatosis, but I loved rabbits. We kept the pair until there were kits, then gave the breeding pair to a friend. I kept one, 'Weanling', as a pet, along with the poddy lambs, piglets, and Seamus the kid goat. Pigeons were added to the menagerie as well. The horses came next.

The winds of change kept blowing, sometime just a gentle breeze other times almost a gale. We had settled into a routine and the boys were growing up fast. Technology was evolving, adding machines had become calculators, students were using scientific calculators at school and wanted personal computers. Brenton got his first, a MicroBee, he played games and started to write programs. At work computers were introduced as well, MS Dos the operating system. I got the task of coding and data entry, something new to make life interesting. The typewriter was put away and the word processor took over.

Then one day I fell in love, a client brought his dog in for treatment, a first-time patient. I first saw a shaggy face with big brown eyes looking over the reception desk at me, the dog standing on his hind legs was as tall as the man leading him in. It was the sweetest most handsome dog I'd ever met; I was sure of that. After the professional part of proceedings had been taken care of (the dog had cut its paw while running along the beach and was admitted for sutures) and as the owner was leaving, I couldn't help myself and said, if ever you need a home for that dog, please think of me. He said that would be most unlikely as it was a prize-winning show dog. Later Mick happened to meet him through a mate. One day he came home and told me that he had been approached by someone who had a Scottish Deer Hound and was looking for a home for it. I asked what sort of dog it was, not knowing the breed, when he explained I agreed it would be nice to have a dog again.

The following weekend a couple arrived with McDuff, my prize-winning show dog. I was ecstatic, I'd known he was meant to be mine; he stood beside me and didn't turn a hair as they drove off. He'd disgraced himself they said; they'd decided to get a giant schnauzer, McDuff fell out of favour, and all the attention went to the new dog. Then one day the dogs met face to face, McDuff gave it a hiding, after all he'd been top dog for years. Now poor McDuff was a shadow of his former self, covered in fleas with allergy sores, muscles wasted from lack of exercise and hipbones showing through his thinning coat. It took almost six months to get him back to health, Mick must have all the credit for exercising and getting him fit again. He took him on long walks, then on the bike, leading him on the leash, finally down to the beach so he could run free, and could he run! It was pretty to watch. Yet he was my dog, my shadow. When we took him down to a friend's farm where we often went with the boys so they could go hunting, we learnt that the dog suffered from agoraphobia, he panicked when out in the open and just lay down. He was fine down at the beach, but hopeless out in the paddocks. That didn't matter to me, I was perfectly happy to have him as a house dog.

Paul asked for a cricket team for Christmas but had to settle for a cricket set. No-one knows how many overs Brenton bowled to him that summer. The neighbour had built a cricket practice net which was very convenient. We gave Brenton an air rifle, we never had a fear of guns, they were part of life, a tool to be used like any other, with care, when and if needed. Years earlier Mick had purchased two Brno .22 rifles, one for each of the boys, and put them away. The air rifle was the first step in learning about shooting. He had taught me to use a rifle and revolver shortly after we met, now was the time to educate the boys. They both learnt well and were good shots. Brenton went on to become an excellent marksman and later won many competitions at target shooting.

Brenton graduated from high school, he was offered a place at UWA to study architecture, as proud parents we were excited to think our son would be a university graduate one day, following his grandfather's profession. In 1974 the Whitlam Labour Government had abolished tuition fees for students at university, my mother and her friend Josef were happy for him to come and live with them, we would sort everything out before the first term was due to start. Josef was keen to have him, said that he would be happy for Brenton to work with him in the butchering-smallgoods business during his free time so that he could be earning. Brenton had a talent for drawing and design, he'd said he wanted to do industrial design and was disappointed with the offer.

He enlisted in the Army instead. I had attended careers counselling with him during his last year at high school, the recruiting officer sold the career well. Brenton at age 17 left for Victoria, to Kapooka for basic training, followed by Corp training and was posted to Bendigo, his rank 'Sapper', his trade 'photographic technician' in the Survey Unit. Paul still at high school, played football in winter. He was winning competitions in surf lifesaving. Both of them strong and healthy young men.

Over the past few years, I'd felt that Mick and I had begun to drift apart, ships in the night, so busy that we were walking down parallel paths, the pressures of work and raising a family was taking a toll. Our social group seemed to be going the same way, was that how middle age changes you? Mick was having difficulties at work, the routine and the hard physical aspect of it, his body was rebelling, he was often in pain. Old injuries were coming back to haunt him (he'd suffered a serious back injury before I'd met him, a riding accident, it had taken 12 months for him to recover, he still carried the scars) his hands were being impacted by RSI from lengthy periods of clipping hooves during the sheep foot rot eradication program, catching and tipping sheep checking for lice aggravated his back. He'd been passed over for promotion, his lack of formal education now making his life difficult. Everyone needed Diplomas now, practical experience counted for little, part of the changing world we were living in.

The eighties were the BIG years in Australia, (also known as the "Greed Decade") everything was big, a time of boom-and-bust cycles, political, technological, economic, cultural and demographic factors wrought significant change. Corporate take-overs, tax evasion through creative schemes, one dubbed the "Bottom of the Harbour Scheme". Mining, merchant banking and media were mentioned in the daily news. OPEC raised oil prices generating a soaring demand for coal. It was also a remarkable decade of film, television, theatre, music and literature. The big share-market crash, big economic reforms and painful adjustments.

It was the decade that transformed Australia. It was perhaps the most controversial decade in Australian history, with high-flying entrepreneurs booming and busting, torrid debates over land rights and immigration, the advent of AIDS, a harsh recession. It was a time when Australians fought for social change on picket lines, at rallies for women's rights, against nuclear weapons and as part of a new environmental movement. Inflation and interest rates were dreadfully high during the eighties, fluctuating between 5 and 10%, our home loan rate peaked at 18%, effectively extending our ten-year term by an additional four years. It was an expensive time to have a mortgage. Wages couldn't keep up with rising costs. It was the recession 'we had to have' according to our treasurer Paul Keating, were we really on the road to becoming a "banana republic"?

Although wages increased, so did costs, stretching our budget was becoming more challenging, I started to bake our bread again, Mick would buy a beast at the cattle sales and have it processed at the local meat-works, then bring it home as quarter beef, we would convert our garage into a butchering shop, bone out the meat, make sausages and mince. Portion every cut four ways, then share the cost with three other families. It certainly brought the price of meat down for all of us. Our vegetable garden and fruit trees were productive and our chickens kept us in eggs. We purchased potatoes by the bag, direct from farmers, started to frequent used clothing stores for suitable garments, patched and mended our clothes, even re-soled our shoes just as father had done when I was small. It all helped to ease the strain on our finances. I was working at two jobs, days at the vet clinic and I had taken on an evening job to help out a friend who had been diagnosed with lung cancer and was no longer able to work. After she died, I spent time training her replacement at the business to take over the role. I was very sorry for her and her family, her husband became a lost soul keeping the business running, whilst putting on a brave face. Mick had been working shifts at a local hotel just to earn a few extra dollars, doing security, American servicemen were coming to Bunbury for R&R so there were some lively nights on occasion.

Our horses were a shared interest. Mick had an owner-trainer licence and was training a couple of race horses, one had leukaemia and had to be retired. He borrowed a brood mare and put her to stud, she had a male foal, unfortunately the foal never saw the track. Then we purchased a brood mare, a gentle soul, she didn't get pregnant but 'China Doll' was a lovely hack for me to ride. I accompanied Mick when he was getting his gelding Pirate Prince ready for a race or event. Brenton went along as his strapper while he was still at home. Then Mick retired Pirate Prince from racing. The daughter of a friend rode him for show jumping for a time. She was only a beginner and the horse was too strong for her so he came back to our stable soon after.

When Paul had graduated from high school he elected to go and work at Worsley Alumina, he had mates working there and followed suit. Paul started competing in endurance events, Avon River Descent, Bridge to Bridge paddle and surf carnivals. The Surf Club entered a team in the Blackwood Marathon, they needed a horse and rider. Paul did the kayak paddle; Mick rode Pirate Prince in the horse leg. The following year the Club entered two teams; I rode China Doll. The weather was foul that year, driving rain and freezing wind, my mare slipped on a flat granite outcrop and went down, I came off and was rather bruised for a few weeks but not seriously injured. The mare wasn't hurt which was a great relief. The previous year it had been so hot we feared for Pirate's welfare. We didn't compete anymore after that, just rode for pleasure, eventually turned the horses out into an agistment paddock.

Mick faced personal tragedies during those years. He lost his father to a fatal heart attack. I've previously mentioned his parents had settled at Binningup. His father had once again come out of retirement and was working for an architectural firm in Bunbury. Sadly, he died while at his drawing board. A while later we got word that his brother had been injured in a road accident in the Adelaide Hills. His daughters had to make the awful decision to turn off the life support. It was a sad, awful time. His niece Bridget and her little son Luke came and stayed with us for a few weeks, it was nice to get to know her as an adult and learn about her and the family. We hadn't seen them since our last visit to Adelaide when Brenton was small. Mick made two trips back to the Northern Territory for funerals, a close friend died when the helicopter he was in during a feral animal cull went down, and again when his old boss from the AIB died, he said that although it was sad to be burying his mates, the reunions with mates and colleagues was good.

Brenton came home to us on leave a couple of times, it was lovely to see him. We still did the same things but he was different, not a child anymore, he'd moved on with his life taking a different direction. I travelled back to Bendigo with him, we enjoyed the trip, camping out along the way, it was great seeing where he was working and living. Bendigo is a lovely city with a lot of history. The following year Brenton's son Matthew was born, his mother a Bunbury local girl who had gone to Victoria for work where they met up again. I was in my fortieth year and a grandmother. It made me happy and so was Mick, being a grandfather suited him. The relationship between Matthew's parents faltered and they ultimately went separate ways, we stayed in touch with his mother and saw Matthew from time to time, although not often. The following year Brenton announced his engagement to a young woman serving in the same army unit, they married in Bendigo with their army friends as attendants.

Paul was still living at home part time, he was considering his long-term career options and started to think about the Army as well. He applied and was accepted to the military college Duntroon, in Canberra. It didn't take him long to realise that a military career wasn't for him so he applied to be discharged. Meanwhile Brenton and his wife had decided to try their luck in the civilian world and left the Army, returning to Western Australia. Brenton began to study architectural drafting. Mick and I carried on as before accepting each change and dealing with every challenge that cropped up. We had a nice circle of friends and spent free time with our horses and dogs.

In 1988 we went back to the Northern Territory for a holiday, it was a wonderful trip up through the interior of Western Australia to Kununurra, then into the Northern Territory to Darwin and Katherine, where we visited old friends and favourite places, we parked outside our old home in Darwin, momentarily re-lived the awful event of Cyclone Tracy, then drove away. The house hadn't been re-built, the screening around the piers made up the walls of the residence, the stairs still led up to the 'Dancefloor'. Mick's mate had purchased a property near Katherine. While we were visiting, coincidentally he'd arranged a helicopter muster to clear the last of the wild cattle off the property, I got to ride in the bull-catching wagon and Mick managed the yards as the cattle were brought in. I felt 16 again, picturing myself on the film set of the movie *"Hatari"*, the only thing missing was the soundtrack, it was exhilarating. We drove back to Western Australia taking the inland route through Top Springs to Halls Creek and then followed the coast road back to Bunbury.

I guess that's where the idea to leave the day-to-day routine of suburban life and return to the outback was rekindled. Mick was hating the routine of daily life more and more, my job was becoming repetitive and mundane, perhaps I was ready for a change as well, although torn at the thought of leaving our home and Paul behind. The deciding factor ultimately was the news that Mick was to be transferred to Katanning or Lake Grace at the start of the new year. Both predominantly sheep areas, where he was expected to oversee the foot-rot eradication program. He discussed his concerns with his doctor and his supervisor, his doctor had written a report stating how detrimental it would be to his health, he'd turned fifty that year. The Department was adamant that the transfer would go ahead, citing that Mick had signed an agreement when he commenced working with them, that he was prepared to be posted wherever they deemed necessary. It took two phone calls for him to secure employment in Queensland on the Wild Dog Barrier Fence.

Decision time for me; Mick was due to start in two months' time, he'd given me the option to come with him or stay in Western Australia until Paul was more settled. I did a fair bit of soul searching. Our sons were independent young men, did the security of the brick and tile house, my job and the life I'd come to know mean that much? Did Paul need a minder? My beautiful McDuff was no more, he'd been bitten by a dugite, we had spent hours trying to save him, I'd seen his spirit leave his body, he was buried in the garden, along with Pusscat, Yarloop, the ferrets, Weanling my rabbit had succumbed to myxomatosis, Toulouse our rooster had passed on one night by the back door and turned into a pile of feathers.

Perhaps it really was time, the wind of change had been getting stronger, we only had 'Victor' the Blue Heeler pup now. Being with Mick was the most important thing in my life, my future was with him. Ready for new horizons and whatever life had to offer I resigned my job and bought an Akubra hat, friends gave me a pair of Blundstone boots. The people at work gave me a radio-CD player, a useful gift for where we were heading.

In record time we packed up, bought a caravan, gave away what we didn't really need, sold the cars and bought a Falcon Ute, put the house on the rental market. Said our goodbyes, one of our neighbours in wishing us well said he was sure we would soon be surrounded by animals again, glad that he had built the cricket nets and our sons had enjoyed them as much as his boys did. On the morning of our twenty third wedding anniversary we pulled out of the driveway with our dog Victor and my canary 'Flipper Parrot', ready to start the new decade in Thargomindah, Queensland.

We left with very little. Paul said to us that there was something weird about the move, saying "Isn't customary for the children to leave home, not the parents". I told him my future was with his father, he was an adult now and knew how to stand on his own two feet. I felt confident that with family support all would be well. My sister, her husband David, their grandmother, as well as some of our friends would look out for our sons and be there for them if anything untoward should happen. After all we were only moving interstate, not to the other side of the world, as our parents had done.

Some significant events of the decade were:

- A severe hail storm in Brisbane and surrounding areas in Queensland caused extensive damage.
- The Ash Wednesday Bush-fires in Victoria.
- The introduction of Medicare.

- The stopping of the Franklin River Dam project, saving a key wilderness area in Tasmania.
- The bicentenary of the founding of Australia by the First Fleet.
- The inventions of the internet, DNA profiling, the nicotine patch, the MIR Space Station.
- The Iran-Iraq War, the Falklands War and the Lebanon War.
- The Chernobyl disaster.
- The Exxon Valdez oil spill.

7

Then the Parents Left Home

The trip across the Nullarbor was an adventure holiday, a second honeymoon. We admired the ever-changing scenery, stopped for meal breaks and night camps. The canary sang his little heart out each time we stopped and I brought him out into the sunshine. The pup sniffed around and stretched his legs. We headed up to Broken Hill from Port Augusta, along the Barrier Highway to Bourke, then Goondawindy into Queensland, up to St George and turned west, passed through Cunnamulla, continuing on towards Thargomindah.

Perhaps leaving Western Australia should have been more of a wrench, I didn't feel it. We'd had plenty of time to talk and rediscover what had brought us together at the beginning, our relationship had changed but we still shared the same dreams and sense of adventure. We found each other again. Mick had spent part of his youth in the Channel Country, the area we were heading to and I felt safe and started to look ahead.

Thargomindah, a small town, isolated, at the end of the railway line, further west there was just the expanse of the Australian inland. We booked into the Caravan Park, hung the bird cage up and decided to go for a walk down to the Bulloo River. Not a good start I'm sorry to say, when we got back my little bird had been eaten by a cat. A wave of emotion overcame me, the enormous change I was facing was too much after all. I cried a bucket of tears, Mick tried to comfort me, but in the end, he had to just let me be. I suddenly felt ill with homesickness for the life we'd built and left behind, and sadness for the loss of all our pets that lay buried. Felt that I'd deserted our sons, young and impetuous. I felt very small and alone. Suddenly frightened of what lay ahead and full of doubt as to whether I could adapt. That little foreign girl tended to rise up whenever I least expected it. After a while the flood stopped and Mick and I went into the little town and had a meal at the pub. The supervisor was coming down from Quilpie to meet us next day and take us out to the Barrier Fence Camp which would be our base.

* * *

Thargomindah

Thargomindah and our run on the barrier fence certainly were a new experience, there was 460km of fence to maintain, the longest section. The camp was at the half-way point of the run, some distance out of town, at a station bore. The camp consisted of a fenced compound with a wire store and a rudimentary demountable cabin, outside shower under an overhead water tank and the unenviable long-drop dunny. Fortunately, the demountable had an indoor shower and flushing toilet. A kitchen and bunkroom. There was no shade. The demountable had gaslights, a half size gas fridge and twin-burner gas stove, with a griller oven. No generator to power our caravan. We made that a priority purchase along with a twin tub washing machine. The section of fence we would be patrolling ran from the New South Wales border to Windorah. Water was pumped into the overhead tank via a windmill from the station bore. The patrol schedule was one week south, the following week north.

The vehicle supplied was a four-wheel drive Mitsubishi Triton Ute, fitted with a rack carrying rolls of netting and coils of wire, jerrycans for fuel and water, a small 12-volt fridge, a trailer, an assortment of tools, a rifle and chainsaw. The trailer served to carry our camping gear and other necessities, there was room on the back of the Ute for the dog. Importantly a two-way radio as a lifeline, no mobile phones out there yet. We added the canopy from our Falcon Ute to provide shade for our dog.

The supervisor took Mick on a patrol down to the border and back along the road network, then up to the meeting camp at the northern end, and back through Eromanga, I stayed behind and set up our camp. It was assumed that I would be accompanying Mick on the patrols as the other runs were staffed by 2-man teams. This one however had always been a husband-and-wife team, although only one was on the payroll. There was a depot at Quilpie which had earth moving equipment and a 'Flying Gang' who would assist in the event of a flood or other disaster bringing the fence down, and for any section upgrades. The fence ran through a number of sheep stations, its purpose was to prevent wild dogs and dingoes from gaining access to and attacking sheep. The other side of the fence was mostly cattle country. They also employed a "Dogger" whose job it was to drive the length of the fence and lay baits.

The history of the Australian Dingo Fence is interesting in itself, one of the longest structures in the world, three times longer than the Great Wall of China. It stretches some (3,488 miles) 5,614 kilometres. From its origin west of the Eyre Peninsula on the cliffs of the Nullarbor Plain above the Great Australian Bight (near Nundroo) in South Australia, it meanders north-east across the State through thousands of kilometres of arid country until it reaches the New South Wales border, then heading north following the state border to Cameron Corner where it turns east. At Hamilton Gate it turns north into Queensland. At Windorah it turns east again, then continues to meander through the sheep grazing country and eventually peters out past Roma near the town of Chinchilla, then on to Jimbour not quite reaching Dalby. There is a lot written about it and it's a source of adventure for many people who follow it in order to explore the inland of our great land.

Although it has reached icon status, I feel it is an environmental disaster. It upsets the balance of nature; it interrupts the migration habits of our native animals and excludes dingoes who are the natural predator, no longer keeping population numbers in check. Population numbers explode in good seasons, the animals die horribly during droughts, unable to reach fodder and water through migration. Small creatures are trapped in the wire, birds and reptiles especially. Feral pigs, goats, and rabbit numbers are seasonally out of control. Baiting programs kill other fauna and the number of shooters harvesting feral animals barely make an impression. I don't have the answers as to how to manage the problem and keep the livestock safe, but feel there must be another way.

It was getting hot by the end of November in 1989. In order to improve our camp Mick and I built a bough shed to protect our Ute. Built a landing with hand rail and awning over the door to the demountable using bush timber, wire netting reeds and leaves for the thatched roof. Planted some lawn (water couch) between the demountable and our caravan, laid a gravel path, put up a small fence around an area for a vegetable garden and set up a makeshift laundry on pallets by the overhead tank stand.

We had to flood irrigate the lawn and vegetables as the bore water was so alkaline it would burn the plants if it got on the leaves and could eat away a waterbag within a week. There was a lot of good mulch from debris washed up against the fences, it contained lots of rabbit, 'Roo and sheep manure so would grow good veggies. I planted petunias and sunflowers as well as vegetable seedlings. I learnt about adding gypsum to the soil, this opened up the clay particles and allowed air and water to get to the plant roots. A very useful tip I was most grateful for.

Christmas was extremely hot, we fashioned a footbath using a tarpaulin and sat in the shade of our bough shed with our feet in water to escape the heat during the day, the police constable from Thargomindah spent the day with us, as his wife had taken the children to stay with her parents in Brisbane for the holidays. Our camp stools and folding table served us well for Christmas lunch. By night we ran our generator to cool the caravan so we could sleep. It was so hot that crows were literally dying from heat stress and birds were dropping out of the sky, the lucky ones found water and shade.

Our hottest day that summer was 50°c in the demountable, it may well have been hotter but the thermometer couldn't go any higher, it was 10pm when we got back to the camp. It was still so hot that the vehicle had kept boiling driving over the De-Grey Range and even after sundown we had to keep stopping so the radiator could cool, we had spent the afternoon sitting in a waterhole in a creek on Nockatunga Station shaded by coolabah trees and wrapped in wet blankets, the hot wind sucking them dry in record time. The dog had sat in the water as well with just his nose out for most of the time. We set up our shearer's beds on our wet lawn and slept under the stars after drinking a couple of cold beers at 2am.

I had brought a camera to record the images of what we would see in this part of Australia. I became a shutter-bug wanting to share it all with my family. The country was beautiful, beyond description, the colours of sunrise and sunset, the wildlife and the vegetation. A dead mulga tree could look like it had come to life with the number of budgerigars sitting on the boughs, green and gold, their plumage shining in the sunlight. There were flocks of exotic colourful parrots and Gouldian finches, majestic wedgetail eagles, who built nests in the mulga tree tops, piled high with rabbits to feed their young. Reptiles, kangaroos, wallabies and emus, dad leading his young striped chicks and sounding like a motor bike being kickstarted during the mating season. The flora was just as beautiful and enchanting, Leopardwood, brigalow, bloodwood, mulga, quandong and eucalypts, just to name a few. The groundcovers and shrubs flowering red, white, cream, lavender and yellow, plants and wildflowers all so spectacular, native pasture of button grass, bluegrass and fluffy clumps of Kangaroo and Wallaby grass.

The strange smell of the brigalow after rain, the sparks of bloodwood timber in a campfire, lignum growing in the swampy ground, gidgee coals glowing so intensely and giving off such heat that they had inspired poets. There was one section of the fence where the track veered away from the fence, the only way to check it was to walk. As I came up out of the ravine into a clump of mulga trees a flock of the most colourful parrots took to the air, the ground beneath was covered in maidenhair ferns, it was quite enchanting. The ever-changing terrain, from red to black soil, ochre-coloured cliffs overlooking deep ravines, gibbers and opal thunder eggs. If you were lucky, they split to reveal a heart of amazing colour. Creek beds with colourful agate washed and polished by nature. Outcrops of pure white quartz, seamed with fool's gold. Flowing artesian bores, the water so hot the houses in town had cooling tanks on the roof. I took dozens of photos none of which did justice to what I was actually seeing.

At the end of summer, the rains came, and didn't stop, Charleville was flooded, there was water everywhere, the creeks, channels and rivers flooded, we were rained in. We'd had a number of quite severe thunder storms and a few close calls, almost getting stranded. We'd got bogged on a black-soil plain and narrowly avoided disaster. The vehicle was jacked up in order to get logs under the wheel so we could drive out, the jack tilted and the vehicle came down trapping Mick's hand. I learnt to use a Wallaby Jack in a hurry that day, Mick stayed calm and talked me through the procedure. He went very pale and I knew he was in trouble, afterwards he said the pain and panic he was feeling was overwhelming. He had to tolerate my driving for the rest of the day, we made it home to base. During flood isolation Mick would go out on foot to hunt, (even the three-wheeler motorbike got bogged, the red soil was suddenly bottomless) there was nothing, all the animals had scattered. Fortunately, we had a good store of supplies.

We read everything we had at least twice; I unravelled a pullover just to pass the time by re-knitting it. Mick did wood carving and plaited leather boot laces into a belt. One day he walked to the main road to check on our mail, came back with a long postage tube, it was full of Easter eggs. Brenton had sent them to us. I hope he knows how much we appreciated the gesture. Then finally we heard a vehicle, the manager from the station we were based on came to check on us, he'd made a track to the main road and we could finally venture out again. The country dried out as quickly as it had flooded. There was a lot of damage to the fence, we were kept busy for quite some time. The sandfly plague that followed the flood was something else again. The poor animals could get no respite, kangaroos were dying from stress. The feral pigs were having a field day, there were wallows galore and they walked under the fence like it wasn't there. Then the pig hunters came out from town, set up a portable chiller and the cull began.

Winter gets cold out there, we still camped out most nights and were grateful for our little tent, it had kept the flies and mosquitoes at bay and now served to protect us from the cold wind and frost. We had made friends with a number of the station folk along our run and were often invited to come in to the homestead for a meal and to stay the night. We were over at one of the stations to watch the NRL grand final, their little daughter was very sick with 'flu. I held the child while her mother packed a bag getting ready for the Flying Doctor who was coming to take them to Charleville Hospital. Happily, the little girl recovered. I had the worst bout of 'flu that winter, the only time I missed going on patrol with Mick.

The Dogger was active on our section, our dog Victor almost became a casualty of 10-80 poisoning. The Dogger was not supposed to bait along the track as baits get caught in tyres and farm working dogs could accidentally eat one. He was also meant to notify anyone known to be using the track that he was working in the area. We were always vigilant whenever Victor was off the vehicle, as these 'factory' baits last for years. On this occasion we stopped to close off a section where pigs had pushed through. Victor jumped down when he wasn't meant to, Mick saw him pick something up right by the Ute, grabbed him and forced his jaw open, sure enough a crunched-up factory bait, still in its wrapper, they look like honeycomb. Mick scooped out what he could, I grabbed a water bottle and we flushed his mouth.

Hearts racing and fingers crossed we hoped for the best. He seemed okay when we turned in for the night, in the morning he had a fit and screamed, wrapped his front paws around Mick's legs and it happened again. A sound you don't want to ever hear again. Mick told me to go and get the rifle, saying if he does it again, we'll have no option but to let him go, "I can't let him die like that", he said. It happened three times, then he settled trotted off and did what a dog needs to do, he seemed to recover. I'm guessing he wondered why he got so much special treatment after that and was tied up on the back, only allowed down under full supervision. Mick didn't mince his words and the 'Dogger' was left in no doubt about his personal pedigree after that, we never met up with him again.

We'd taken a trip to Tibooburra one weekend and met up with the supervisor of the New South Wales Wild Dog Exclusion Fence. By the end of September of that year we'd secured a position with the 'Wild Dog Destruction Board' on their section of the fence. The runs were shorter and the job came with a cottage. We gave notice, said our goodbyes and headed off to Longreach. We were in no rush so travelled along at a leisurely pace, camping in our van nightly. We were getting low on supplies so one evening while at a waterhole tried our luck fishing, only thing we caught was a tortoise which we returned to the river. We dug for mussels in the mud of the bank, cleaned them in salted water. I made a light batter of flour and water, we fried them in some mutton fat, served them up with salt, pepper and tomato sauce on a slab of damper. I can honestly say it was one of the worst meals I have ever eaten. Beaten only perhaps by an insipid vegetable soup made from powdered milk and a can of mixed vegetables. Victor was eating 'road kill', we usually managed to find a fresh kill early most mornings to meet his needs.

The Stockman's Hall of Fame had been built in Longreach, and the last Cattle Drive had taken place, a big celebration was planned. Mick was invited as an honoured guest for his contribution to the cattle industry and we were told his story would be recorded for posterity. It was also an opportunity to catch up with old friends who would be there from the Territory. We'd had an enjoyable leisurely trip, stopping at Blackhall (home of the famed Jackie Howe, the 'gun' shearer, and Barcaldine, birthplace of the Australian Labor Party, and famed for the Shearer's Strike, arriving just in time for a Country Music Muster. Then we continued on to Longreach, home of the Qantas Museum, School of the Air, Flying Doctor and Captain Starlight, the notorious cattle thief, who bested the desert and the law and was found 'not guilty' at the court sitting in Roma by his peers, 'Banjo' Patterson country, he allegedly wrote his famed poem 'Waltzing Matilda' while visiting the area. We decided to camp down by the Thompson River.

The reunion was a grand affair, the stockmen and drovers were registered and interviewed, their stories recorded. We met many of Mick's former colleagues and friends, yarns and stories were regaled, lots of photos taken and contact details exchanged. An afternoon of fancy horse riding was the entertainment, a BBQ and country music night followed. Next day after a BBQ breakfast, when all the speeches had been made and official photos taken, people started to disperse. One of Mick's mates tried hard to place me, sure we had met somewhere before, I'd recognised him immediately, he had been a patient when I was a trainee nurse. On the second day he remembered where he knew me from, then he told us about the "Black Dog" that had marred his life. He had been brought to Australia as a child from the UK presumed to be an orphan, grown up at Bindoon 'Boys Town', a farm and trade school run by the Christian Brothers in Western Australia, only there was no Christianity to be found there, the children were treated in the most appallingly cruel manner. [3] He had left as soon as he was old enough and found work in the stock camps of northern Australia. The horrors of his early life never left him, at times the darkness overwhelmed.

---

[3] Bindoon Boys Town: The sad truth behind Britain's lost children. An appalling, notorious place. (Reference; article by Kathy Marks – Independent.co.uk 06/09/2009)

The poor man poured his heart out to us, he had married and had a family but the marriage had broken down, he gave us his daughter's address and asked if we would send the photos of this happy weekend to him there. We spent the rest of the day on the bank of the Thompson River fishing in a picnic atmosphere, old mates together. Then the party was over. We sent the photos to him at his daughter's address, she wrote to us thanking us, said she would treasure them, he never received them, he left this life shortly after the Drover's Reunion, the "Black Dog" had won.

At the end of 1989 we left Western Australia to start our new life in Queensland, looking back now in 1990, so much had happened in the previous decade on the world stage:

- The Berlin Wall had come down and Germany was unified again.
- There had been a Royal Wedding.
- Australia had won the 'America's Cup' with the revolutionary 'Winged Keel' designed by Ben Lexcen.
- The disasters of Tiananmen Square.
- The Space Shuttle *'Challenger'* explosion.
- The Mount St. Helen's volcanic eruption.
- Our national heroes were our cricketers, especially Dennis Lillee, I can almost still hear the chanting of his name.

We decided to head back to the west to visit family and check on our house, having learnt that the tenant had moved on and the property was vacant again. We left our caravan in Broken Hill and headed west.

A safe and uneventful trip back. Barbara and her husband David were settled in their lovely home at North Lake. Mother living in a unit in a retirement village nearby. Brenton was pursuing his studies. Paul working back at Worsley Alumina on a new career path, still playing football and recently returned from a trip to Thailand. The house needed a bit of work which we took care of. Traded our Ute on a four-wheel drive Toyota Land Cruiser. Paul and his mate moved into our house. We had a combined birthday and early Christmas dinner hosted by my sister Barbara and David, all our family were together for the occasion, then we once again said our farewells.

We left Bunbury at sun-up, again heading east across the Darling Escarpment, through farmland of wheat and sheep, reaching the start of the Nullarbor Plain by evening, we found a suitable camp site and settled for the night. I enjoyed the journey each time we made the crossing, never tiring of the scenery and being amazed at the vistas. Reaching the Flinders Ranges in South Australia signalled that we really were about to embark on a new adventure.

***

Tibooburra and Bindara Gate

We arrived in Broken Hill to collect our caravan, this time heading north to Tibooburra and the next chapter on the Dog Fence, based at Bindara Gate. Each of the patrol stations along the New South Wales fence had a gate, if the emu migration or kangaroo numbers got too great and put pressure on the fence the gate could be opened, the animals let through to continue on their natural migration paths. It was also convenient to be able to patrol the fence from both sides.

I was following in the footsteps of Burke and Wills into my next unknown. We stopped in town and met with the supervisor and his wife, staying overnight. Next day he escorted us out to Bindara Gate, we bypassed Wompah Gate where the foreman was based and passed by Adelaide Gate (this cottage was now deserted) and onwards. Having traversed a stony plain, all the while fearing for our caravan while it bounced over the rocks, we now came to a cane-grass floodplain, the watershed of the Bulloo River. Next, we went over large red sandhills until we reached Bindara Gate cottage. Mick parked the van in front of the cottage. The supervisor and Mick headed off to inspect the section of fence that we would be responsible for, while I was left to have a look around. Quite dumbfounded at what confronted me.

There was a Suzuki Ute parked in front of the cottage; this was the Dog Board vehicle fitted out with a two-way UHF radio. A tall radio mast stood by the corner of the cottage, it was for the VHF radio set, communication to the Flying Doctor base in Broken Hill, doubling as a swing for a flock of cockatoos. I'm not really sure where to start or how to describe the state of the cottage. The dog-board compound was sited in a square mile horse paddock, there was an airstrip, a large dam with a smaller silt-catch dam connected by a flume near the top of the dam wall, (a series of concrete pipes approximately a metre in diameter) so that only clean water was stored. The catchment drains were so silted that they were barely discernible. The silt-catch dam was almost dry, cracked drying mud visible in the bottom along with the carcasses of unfortunate creatures who had gone into the mud looking for water. The main dam didn't have much water in it either. The windmill wasn't turning, there was no wind. I hoped the overhead tank wasn't empty. The cottage was surrounded by a circular corrugated iron fence with numerous missing panels, circular so that no matter which way the wind blew the sand during a storm didn't pile up and bury it or push the fence over.

The four-room cottage was set on stumps, another Williams hut, steel framed, corrugated iron clad building, a verandah on all four sides. The verandah was wrapped with shade-cloth and divided into the following; On the front to the left side of the main door was an office, containing the VHF radio sitting on the Flying Doctor emergency medical chest. On the rear verandah, to the left of the kitchen door a screened meat-room, to the right a store room with shelving, a bathroom (shower over bath) basin and a separate WC. Between the rear of the office and meat room was a workbench set against the side of the kitchen wall. Everything was covered in a layer of sand; I left footprints as I walked around. Pairs of house martens had mud-nests in the rafters. I entered the interior of the cottage with trepidation; the bedrooms and kitchen had 2 windows each.

The living room had an open fireplace, a window overlooking the front verandah, in addition to the main entrance, there were doorways to the kitchen and front bedroom. The kitchen was fitted out with a wood stove and sink in one corner, a new gas fridge, a table and 4 chairs (in poor condition) and a kitchenette unit. the walls and ceiling in every room were blackened with years of smoke buildup. The floor boards throughout were bare, the front and back doors aligned to create a breezeway. (A walk-through passage or 'dog trot'.)

In the centre of the ceiling in each room was a square screened vent, a single bare light bulb hung from the middle of it. Access to the second bedroom was from the kitchen. Outside the back door were two rainwater tanks. A divided out-building contained on one side a laundry with a kerosene refrigerator, a copper and two cement wash tubs. A generator, a bank of batteries, a diesel drum and pump were in the other section with a couple of oil drums and a family of shingle-back goanas. The cement slab floor was so thick with sand and oil it looked like a dirt floor. A donkey boiler sat between the laundry and bathroom for hot water. Three stunted Athel pine trees completed the picture. To further enhance and frame this vista the paddock outside was strewn with an assortment of wrecked vehicles. Piles of fencing material and empty fuel drums. The only useful thing I could see was a fenced chicken coop which I thought would make a good vegetable garden. The presence of many rabbit warrens and rabbits running around in daylight warning me of the need for secure fencing.

The rear bedroom contained a collection of old clothes and assorted belongings piled up on the floor, on the back verandah a pile of rubbish. A tabby kitten made its presence known by twinning around my legs, it looked around eight weeks old, I wondered about the rest of the litter and any other cats. I picked the kitten up intending for it to become part of our 'family', this seemed to be okay for a while but Victor wasn't convinced that it wasn't a rabbit, one day when I wasn't watching he picked it up and bit too hard, heelers have strong jaws, unfortunately the kitten didn't survive.

The smell of carrion was overwhelming. We soon found out that there was a pair of Perente (monitor lizards) living under the cottage, feasting on the rabbits which inhabited the burrows underneath. Thank God for our caravan and generator, our camp beds and washing machine. We were later informed that the kitchenette unit belonged to a family living in Tibooburra, and they had asked to have it brought back into town but for $60 we could have the table and chairs. I said that I would like to have the other belongings removed ASAP and the pile of garbage could go also.

The supervisor Garry apologised for the state of things, explaining that the previous occupant had left in a hurry, convinced that the ghost of Bindara was going to 'get him', after drinking himself into the horrors. No one had been back to clean up. He bagged and took the refuse away with him when he left. Mick and I took stock of our situation and made a plan to sort things out and make it habitable. In the meantime, the caravan would do nicely. We never used the laundry, instead setting our washing machine in the bathroom and rinsing the washing in the bathtub.

We met Godfrey the foreman next day; he eventually took the kitchenette away with him along with the $60 for the table and chairs.

In his pocket was a list for sugar soap, brooms and brushes, paint and rollers, a roll of vinyl floor covering, sufficient for at least 2 rooms and some 'coolie-hat' lamp-shades so that the meagre amount of light would at least be deflected downwards. The 'Flying Doctor' emergency medical chest, which on later examination I found was incomplete and the remaining contents out-of-date, also got replenished.

We did our first patrol of the fence; it was in a similar state to the cottage. Dingoes came nightly to drink at the dam, we certainly had our work cut out for us. Hot doesn't describe conditions out in the inland in summer. Our patrols were done at first light, we were usually back at the cottage by early afternoon, by then the dust was so thick you couldn't see clearly anyway. Dust storms were a regular event, sometimes followed by a rain storm, usually just dry lightning in the distance. Cleaning up afterwards would yield at least a barrow full of sand. Sometimes it would blow all night and by morning the only clean patch in a bed was where you had been laying. We continued to sleep in our caravan.

Brenton had come to Bindara with his wife, to help us get the place organised and have a holiday. On New Year's Eve we had settled out on the cooling sand after sundown to enjoy a few drinks, we could see a storm brewing on the horizon. The indications at this stage were the occasional flashes of lightning. The bulldozer and the drivers mobile camp, were parked up a short distance away from where we were sitting. A bit later in the evening the operator arrived back from a trip to town, we hadn't met him yet, so when he arrived, he came over to us and introduced himself. Bert was quite a typically unique character, not unlike some of the others we had met over the years, out in the isolation of the outback, to escape situations that life had thrown at him. He told us he was from Muswellbrook, a town in the Hunter River region of New South Wales. The storm was getting closer, we could now see the sloping frontline of it, it looked ominous, a big dust storm was certainly heading our way.

We had no option but to retreat to the kitchen and were sitting around the table with mugs of tea when it hit, the lighting from the single bare globe, dim, the batteries had run down, we hadn't run the generator to recharge them that day. Visibility was such in the kitchen that you could barely see across the room. Sand was pouring down the chimney onto the stove-top and raining down through the centre vent of the kitchen ceiling onto the table, it was blowing in under the door and through cracks around the window, we had to put a sheet of paper over our mugs to keep the sand out of the tea. The air was barely breathable. But it was New Year's Eve so we had to do something to celebrate. Bert couldn't get back to his camp anyway, we had a couple of bush poetry books at hand, so we took turns reading Banjo Patterson and Henry Lawson poems. Drinking cool tea and conversing until the storm passed. Happy New Year everyone.

There was magic in that night, it was revealed at daylight, it looked like the world had been reborn, the desert reclaimed by nature, if there was a spirit at Bindara it wasn't malevolent, it was benign. Every footprint and tyre track made by man was erased, the sand around the cottage was calm like wavelets on the ocean on a calm day, just rippled, the air was perfectly still, the sand felt cool on my bare feet. The only signs of life were the scurry marks of lizards, pawprints of rabbits and imprints of bird feet. Birds were sitting around the water's edge of the dam. It was beautiful. With the sun rising and the sky changing colour from pinks and orange to blue it truly was a magic morning. A novel way to start the new year. Later that morning we cleaned up, sweeping buckets of sand out of the cottage.

The paint and vinyl flooring came, we cleaned the walls and painted, laid the flooring. Put our camp beds into the front bedroom. Then we came across a Kookaburra gas cooker in the now deserted cottage at Adelaide Gate and had it installed in the kitchen, it still worked. We called in at Waverley Gate, another deserted cottage and discovered that there were kitchen cabinets. We had them brought to Bindara and suddenly had a workable kitchen. On a trip to Broken

Hill for supplies we bought a secondhand armchair and a small sofa, on the way back Victor settled himself in the chair, laying claim to it, he and Mick regularly battled over that chair.

My mother was coming to visit. It was winter, although cold and windy the best time to visit. We settled her in the caravan and moved into the cottage ourselves. I had made side tables out of paper covered cardboard boxes and a makeshift wardrobe out of the box the gas fridge had come in, so the bedroom and living room were serviceable as well. Brenton and his wife had visited, so did our niece Andrea and her partner from Adelaide, bringing another couple with them. The had chartered a plane and landed on our airstrip, our FIFO visitors. They enjoyed their time in the desert, it being so different from anything they had seen. For us it was a lovely distraction to see them all.

Our vegetable garden was flourishing, I would start the seedlings in Styrofoam boxes on the verandah then plant them out into beds made in what had once been the chook run, our lettuces always had that bit of extra crunch from the top dressing of sand. The zucchini plants were prolific, producing enough to supply our neighbours as well, tomato vines grew tall and I trained them along the netting roof, tomatoes hung down like grapes, root vegetables and brassicas grew just as well, the soil was incredibly rich in minerals and the mulch with natural fertiliser did the rest to feed the plants, all I had to do was add water. Our cottage was further enhanced when we were supplied with an evaporative cooler for the main bedroom and a TV dish. We chose to have ABC TV and QTV from Queensland. Our mail still brought much more than letters; the library bag was always my favourite item. The mail was delivered to the office in Tibooburra, the mail truck brought it out to Wompah Gate. It eventually reached us when the foreman was heading our way, other supplies sometimes came from Wanaaring via Hamilton Gate. We became friends with the boundary riders relying on each other for social activities and assistance if anything went awry.

The following summer was a wet one, the Bulloo River flowed copiously and the watershed was flooded, we were surrounded by an inland sea. It wasn't deep just very wide. We had an amphibian vehicle to patrol the fence in, it was slow but kept us mobile, the dog got so frustrated at times he would jump out and walk. At Easter we had a very unexpected lot of visitors, the water had almost dried up but there were still patches of water and deep mud. A group of four-wheel drive adventurers came up from Sydney, they were told at Hungerford not to go any further, but ignored the advice and continued on. They were well and truly bogged at Adelaide Gate, we were the closest help, Mick assisted to get their vehicles back onto dry ground with the help of his tractor. They spent Easter with us at Bindara Gate, then headed back home. We kept in touch through letters and they came back the following year, this time they left with two of the puppies Victor had sired.

Each morning, we contacted the boundary riders at Hamilton and Wompah Gates to check on each other's welfare. One morning after visiting Hamilton Gate the night before, Mick was asked if he was missing anything, not sure he looked around, Victor was AWOL, one of the dogs at Hamilton Gate was in season, Victor had fallen in love, he had walked back to Hamilton Gate overnight, a distance of 40km, he was sitting with 'Sandshoe,' a border-collie. Mick went to collect him, nine weeks later four puppies arrived. Victor had quite a fan base and all were quickly spoken for. Two were earmarked to go to our new friends in Sydney, the other two became working dogs locally. When the puppies were weaned the two going to Sydney came to stay with us at Bindara until our friends could come and collect them. Victor treated them with disdain, especially when they took over his bed and found his cache of favourite bones, then generally making themselves 'at home'. They were a lot of fun to have around.

One evening while sitting outside on our verandah watching the sunset we noticed a vehicle approaching from an unexpected direction, most of the tourists followed the fence so this was most unusual, the vehicle was coming from the south, along the station track, not at a time of day when the station owner would be out on the run. We soon met our visitors, the man, a Pastor, who with his wife had retired in Wilcannia, a town on the Barrier Highway located on the banks of the Darling River, once the third largest inland port in the country during the river-boat era of the mid-19th century. Now it was just a small town 196km from Broken Hill with a shrinking population, waiting to re-invent itself. They had been missionaries in many parts of the world including South America, where their son and his wife were still living. Now as well as doing charitable work in town, they were travelling around isolated outback stations and gathering oral histories for a book that he planned to write.

Naturally we made them welcome and soon after repeat visits could call them friends. They would let us know when they were coming out, so that we could advise our neighbours, who would gather at our cottage for a pleasant evening, the Pastor would conduct a short service and offer prayers. This was a small comfort to one of the families who had recently suffered a great family tragedy. Their daughter had left their two young grandchildren asleep in the house while she went down to the cattle yards to take smoko to her husband and the stockmen, when they looked back towards the house it was engulfed in flames, before anyone could do anything it was too late, the little ones were lost. How can a family recover from something like this?

After a barbecue meal and camaraderie everyone would return home and our guests settle for the night in our spare bedroom.

One morning at around 4am we heard rustling in the kitchen, our guests were up and huddled by our kitchen stove, we joined them to learn that it was the 'coldest night' they had ever experienced, so cold in fact that some hot tea was all that they could contemplate. It truly does get cold out in the desert as I've said before. The oral histories were documented, Mick told his story of the life of a drover on the road with a travelling mob of cattle, the next time they came he was presented with a draft of his story set out beautifully on cream paper and printed in sepia, with appropriate illustrations. We certainly did meet some truly genuine wonderful people over the years in the outback.

So many more anecdotes, I could go on for hours. The people of the outback are amazing, they are there for many reasons, some to escape the outside world, others born into it, together they form a cohesive unit, always ready to help out and lend a hand. They don't ask 'personal questions', take you at face value, over time they can become your best friends.

The plant operators were a challenge to manage, the grader driver mostly drove around with the blade up or barely topping the track, so the tracks remained rough, the dozer driver didn't like the roly-poly he was supposed to push away from the fence because it got stuck in his tracks, the loader driver who was supposed to put the side brooms on and sweep the sand away from the netting usually tore holes into it, keeping us busy with repairs. The only thing they seemed to really like and had in common was to go to town for a few days and imbibe their favourite brew.

As part of the cleanup around the cottage and house paddock the rolls of netting and wire were neatly stacked together in a single stockpile, the collection of fuel and oil drums neatly lined up, randoms sheets of corrugated iron, steel and wooden fence posts similarly stacked. Then Mick had the dozer driver dig a big pit, push all the wrecks into it, add back-fill then crush the wreckage, then add more back-fill until the ground was level again, the eyesores were all gone. The foreman almost cried next time he came along; he had loved the graveyard of wreckage and mayhem.

Dust storms were a regular event, sometimes just a dusty haze lasting for days, others intense, whole sandhills could be reconfigured, the fence buried completely or previously buried sections exposed. Sometimes the dust would travel and become visible down on the east coast as far away as Brisbane. In the summer the storms could be followed by a rain event, or a dry thunder storm with spectacular lightning displays. The most severe one we experienced lasted for days, it shifted so much sand that the floor of the cottage was completely covered, the verandah almost buried. Brooms weren't much use, shovels had to be used first, then you could sweep the floors. Via the two-way radio someone said that cleaning up was useless, sowing grass seed would make more sense.

Spring was the worst time; the wind didn't seem to stop blowing. The summers were hot, the heat beating down from above and reflecting back off the ground, the mirage shimmered in the distance. The daily weather forecast from Bourke radio never seemed to alter, sounding like a scratched record, repeating while the stylus was stuck in a groove. The weather report daily was 'very warm to hot, with areas of raised dust', the temperature average was 46°C on the verandah.

The dams needed cleaning out and new drains had to be cut. We had been carting water for weeks, either from the flowing bore some distance away on the station or from the dam at Adelaide gate, the final straw was when the Bedford truck slid down the side of the dam we were carting from and practically disappeared. Fortunately, the dozer pulled it out. Mick used the loader and cleaned the silt dam. Then the task of the main dam began, using a scoop bucket attached to cables the dozer and loader were used to scoop out the mud. But our illustrious operators had much difficulty in coordinating the process and seemed unable to communicate their moves resulting in much frustration for Mick, they managed to break the cable at least half a dozen times a day. Between patrolling the fence and trying to get the other jobs like sandhill claying done, he had his hands full.

Eventually the big dam was cleaned out, we had rain, the drains worked and the dams collected water. We could swim to cool off, the water was crystal clear due to the gypsum crystal seams in the soil. It was also 'hard' (alkaline) dried like salt on your skin and your laundry was a stiff as a board when it dried. We used our rainwater sparingly, but had to rinse off with it after washing our hair or swimming. The final rinse for laundry also had to be with rainwater.

Like nature had waved a magic wand the countryside blossomed, green grass appeared almost overnight, the desert bloomed, strawflowers sprang up in gullies, and scrubby little bushes were covered in flowers, wattle and emu bush, (Eremophilla) quandongs and lillypilly. Our neighbours came from Hamilton Gate and collected fresh feed for their horses, just 40km up the road not a drop had fallen. It seemed cruel. The emu migration began and kangaroo numbers seemed to increase. Rabbit numbers exploded, then the shooters followed, setting up camp with their portable chillers, caravans and vehicles equipped with racks, dropdown windshields and spotlights for night shooting. They were a coordinated affair from Mildura, each shooter was allocated a section, there was to be no shooting within our square mile horse paddock. Rabbits had to be head shot, gutted and paired then hung on hooks. All the shooters had to have their rabbits in the chiller by daybreak. One fellow brought his labrador, it saved him getting out to collect his rabbits.

We couldn't trust Victor to do that, once we had hung a pair of rabbits on the hooks on the Suzuki, when we got to camp, we had empty skins, he had eaten the lot. Some shooters put a red film over the light, saying it made the target stand out better. The boundary riders got in on the act, a bit of extra money never went astray. Professionals would bring in up to 200 pair in a night, the best we did was 60 pair, we did have to be up and at work the next morning. The shooters often called at the cottage for a hot drink or to stand by the fire for a bit, it was bitterly cold at night, they fashioned hand covers out of rabbit fur. The meat was going for human consumption and the fur to the hat industry. It was the last time they came, calicivirus had escaped the laboratory and that with myxomatosis put an end to that industry.

The Board decided to replace a particularly bad section of fence so hired a contractor, we all had jobs now. The contractor paid quite well; I must have put thousands of wire ties on that new section. Just to explain, the fence was made up of three types of netting tied to plain wire, a plastic coated reasonably fine mesh went into the ground and was buried, then a waist high section was attached of galvanised chicken wire, the top section was a large mesh bird wire. Posts were 2 meters out of the ground a set distance apart, plain fencing wire was strung at the top, middle and about 30cm above the ground. The mesh was tied at intervals to the wire, the lower wire being the most awkward to tie. I reacted badly to the galvanising on the wire, an allergic reaction caused a nasty rash on my hands. I had a lot of difficulty using my hands for quite a few weeks afterwards from over-using the pliers which had resulted in repetitive strain injury.

The grazier whose property Bindara was on often came and called with a couple of sheep for us, we largely lived on game and home-grown or canned vegetables, and baked our own sourdough bread. A bit of mutton was always welcome. We had bought a smaller generator for me to use in the cottage, the big one powering the caravan, we needed to run the generator for about six hours per day to keep the freezer solid. I had a microwave as well, could use my stand mixer to knead the bread, my sewing machine and iron. The Kookaburra gas stove from Adelaide Gate worked fine so I didn't need to light the wood stove unless it was cold now. The main upside was we had the means to keep fresh meat and pre-prepared meals. The kerosene fridge had done us proud keeping our meat in the past, if the flame was high enough it froze quite well and the gas fridge in the cottage was ok when it wasn't too hot, in really hot weather there wasn't the heat exchange to make it cool properly so Mick's beers were coldest at around 4am.

There was only one medical emergency during our time at Bindara, one of the plant operators slipped on a ladder while attempting to start his generator, which was mounted on a trailer and lost his footing, the metal rung badly lacerated his leg, tearing a large flap of flesh away from the bone. He had been to town and was somewhat worse for wear, told us an elaborate tale of how his injury had occurred. Said a team of shearers were staying at the hotel and had urinated in his bed, when he confronted them, they had cut him. We had to administer first aid, it was a nasty wound and when his 'anesthetic' wore off would be very painful. Mick and his trusty veterinary first aid kit came to the rescue, after sterilising the equipment and cleaning the wound, between us we distracted our patient, using forceps I pulled the flap of flesh back into place, Mick inserted 4 sutures to hold the tissue in place, leaving the bottom of the wound open so excess fluid could drain.

I applied a dressing from the Flying Doctor medical kit and contacted the base in Broken Hill for further instructions and authority to give pain relief to our patient. They said they would send a plane to Tibooburra but we needed to take him in to meet them, I explained that it would be a very uncomfortable trip for the poor fellow, so he was prescribed pain relief. We put a mattress in the back of the Ute for our patient to lay on and headed into town. The Supervisor was coming out to meet us and we would transfer our patient into his care.

All went well and a week or so later our patient was back, he had remembered what had actually happened and told us the true story, said the doctor in Broken Hill was most impressed with Mick's wound care, saving him from needing 'plastic surgery'. The leg soon healed and was as good as new. Some years later I read an article in a magazine, featuring the Flying Doctor Service, it was about the Dog Fence, our illustrious plant operator had been interviewed for a story, he'd painted himself quite a hero with his vivid imagination. The most recent time prior to this, when our veterinary kit had been needed, was for our dog after a tussle with an emu. He'd been wounded when the bird's claw inflicted a nasty looking cut on his chest.

One evening, while sitting around the campfire at Hamilton Gate, Mick mentioned Lake Torrens and the family he had worked for when he was young. The family were originally from this part of New South Wales, from White Cliffs. He wondered where they might be now. The boundary rider Eoin and his wife Fiona were locals, Fiona looked at him intently, asked a couple of questions. It was soon established that the man he was musing about was her cousin and living in Broken Hill. She gave Mick his address and Mick wrote to him, on our next visit to Broken Hill two old friends were reunited. I liked him immediately and he welcomed us both with open arms. We became firm friends. I eventually met other members of his family and we were guests at his daughter's wedding.

Our time at Bindara Gate was drawing to a close, Mick's hands were getting worse and his other scars were making it increasingly difficult to continue with the job. We had to come up with a new plan. We had both studied wool classing by correspondence and Mick was a qualified classer, but travelling from shed to shed following the clip didn't really appeal, I felt it was time to settle somewhere. I'd long had a dream of starting up boarding kennels, a cattery seemed ideal, we discussed it at length, I did up a business plan, it looked good on paper. Our accountant in Broken Hill thought it had merit, or at least would be a nice hobby. The clientele we thought who would use our service were the retirees who had pets, but wanted to travel and young professionals who were in Broken Hill for a short stay, but regularly went back to visit family in the cities.

We listed our house in Western Australia 'for sale' and started looking for a suitable property. The house eventually sold and we found a lovely bluestone Californian style bungalow on the main thoroughfare of Broken Hill. It was on a big block with sufficient room to build the cattery, having good access from the front and a rear laneway. The Council had no objections provided the RSPCA gave us the green light, all the conditions were met and we went ahead with our plan. Catsden Cattery was going to become a reality. This time farewells weren't so final as our fence friends also came to Broken Hill regularly and we would keep in touch.

* * *

Broken Hill - Catsden Cattery

We hired a builder to start on our project. Then Brenton arrived from Leinster, he was looking for a fresh start, he and his wife had found work out in the goldfields but their relationship had floundered, he was about to be single again. It was lovely to have him on board. Mick had several medical reviews and it was deemed he shouldn't be doing manual work; he was granted a pension and collected his superannuation. The cattery was erected, a garage built and a back verandah added to the house. We did some further cosmetic changes and bought some nice furniture, some new and some from the auction house.

Victor had his Bindara chair on the back verandah and a comfortable kennel but usually preferred to sit on the back of Mick's Ute. Business cards were printed and a sign approved for the front lawn. We were open by October; ironically our first client brought his dog to stay at Catsden Cattery. We quickly arranged a kennel with a run so that we could accommodate our guest. That Christmas we had 6 cats boarding, and a budgie hanging on the back verandah. It was a slow start, by the following Christmas we had a full house. We also had a pet turkey in a run and pet rabbit with hutch on the back lawn, numerous birds in cages hanging on the back verandah.

During the winter it was quieter but steady, holiday times people booked in advance to secure a spot. The RSPCA and the local vet referred clients to us. We had an answering machine and a mobile phone so that we were contactable, even outside of business hours. We offered a pick-up and delivery service, then a courier service picking animals up from the airport, boarding them until their people were settled, then delivering them to their new homes. Same when they were ready to return to Adelaide or Sydney. The business was a success, I loved working with the animals and people began to rely on us more and more, it felt like an extended family that kept growing.

Brenton was working casually for the builder who had done our work. He and Mick took up target shooting and travelled to competitions at other rifle ranges, including Adelaide. Both successful and winning often. Mick was concerned for Brenton's future, fearing he would become a drifter unless he found a new career path, they had some serious discussions. Ultimately Brenton applied to re-enlist in the Army and was accepted, he went back to Kapooka and resumed his Army career.

Mick and I took up pistol shooting. At first, I only shot air pistol, then as my skill and passion for shooting grew, participating in all the varied matches on the range. I trained and became a range safety officer, now able to referee and run the club events. I was elected to the committee as treasurer, in addition to my air pistol I now had a .22 Browning semi-automatic with a gold trigger and later a .44 magnum Vaquero revolver. I thoroughly enjoyed my new interest, my favourite event being 'Sports Pistol' now called '25metre Pistol', a 60-shot event, 30 shots in six series of 5 shots, each series 5 minutes and shot on a Precision target, then the rapid-fire stage, 30 shots in six series of 5 shots, each series of 5 exposures of the turning target for 3 seconds, the shooter fires one shot per exposure. The match requiring skill in both precision and rapid fire. For this event I used my .22 Browning semi-automatic. I would often go out to the range early in the morning to practice.

Later we started competing in Western 'Cowboy Action' shooting. It's a competitive shooting sport that originated in the early 1980s in California; it is a multi-gun match using a combination of handguns, rifles and shotguns in a variety of "Old West themed" courses of fire. Participants must dress in appropriate theme or era costumes, as well as use gear and accessories as mandated by the respective sanctioning group rules. Competitors are required to use firearms typical to mid to late 19th century; single action revolvers, lever action rifles, (chambered in pistol calibers) and side by side double barrelled shotguns (coach guns) with or without external hammers. Competitors are required to wear old west style or Victorian fashion outfits and apparel. The one exception is that safety glasses and hearing protection must be worn when shooting. Participants must also select an alias with old west flair – my alias was "Conchita Vaquero". Competition involves a number of separate shooting scenarios, each one different. Targets are typically steel plate that ring when hit. Sometimes reactive steel knock-down plates are used, each scenario is timed and there are penalties for misses or violation. Electronic timers are used. Mick and I also travelled to compete in competitions at other clubs and had our share of success, our collection of embossed glassware grew.

Mick surprised me with a very special birthday gift, he commissioned Pro Hart to paint a picture for me, initially he had wanted a portrait but Pro had said he preferred to paint a scene from one of our 'western action' matches, so this is what I have; a picture depicting me during a match in costume on the range. Such a unique painting done by one of Australia's renowned artists from Broken Hill. Pro (Kevin) Hart was a member of the Pistol Club, he was fun loving and enjoyed the Western Action matches shooting in the Black Powder category so we met often on the range.

The line dancing (Boot Scooting) craze reached Broken Hill, so I dived in head first with a friend, we learnt all the dances, Mick loved the music and watching us have fun so came to all our social events, often filmed our dance demonstrations at shopping centres and other social events. My friend and I entered to dance at the local eisteddfod, I made colourful western style shirts for the occasion, there were entries from all the groups who had sprung up in different parts of the city, we won our division and felt very proud.

We had visitors, our Sydney friends, (bringing the puppies, now lovely dogs) our fence friends were regulars. From family, my mother, sister and her husband, our niece Andrea and her partner, Paul came too, his first visit coinciding with Brenton's march out in Albury-Wodonga. It was a pleasure showing them around, we took them to Silverton, to the sculptures on the hill, and to Wentworth and Menindee Lakes down on the Darling River. The hills and dry creeks all around Broken Hill, all so rugged and harsh in summer but so vastly different after rain, the natural beauty never ceased to amaze me. The business and our weekend activities kept us busy; we enrolled at night classes and did pottery, ceramic studies just for pleasure. Mick's mother died that year, she was an old lady now so it wasn't unexpected but it was a shock nevertheless and he was very sad, both parents and his brother gone. Broken Hill was surrounded by wide open spaces which suited Mick, he didn't feel hemmed in, he got to know the owner of a property on the edge of town, was able to spend time out in the bush, care-taking the station whenever the owners were away, looking after the horses and cattle. It rekindled his dream of a place of his own.

When his mate's property was sold, he was once again at loose ends, missing the station life. I on the other hand had come to love the Silver City, so amazing in so many ways, I even liked the giant mountain of scree that divided north and south. The mining history, the streets named after minerals, the historic buildings, the galleries. The people so down to earth, had embraced us like old friends, supported our business and greeted us wherever we met. It had become home in a very short time.

Brenton came to visit from Queensland, where he was now based, bringing his fiancée Christine to meet us, Paul came too, his visit coinciding with Brenton's. It was always lovely to see our sons. Mick took up .303 rifle shooting with the .303 Rifle Club, established by a group of local ex national servicemen, he stopped shooting big-bore after Brenton left to re-join the army. I joined to keep him company, we had beautiful rifles, Mick had set them up with floating barrels and we loaded our own ammunition. I surprised myself winning the 'inaugural ladies' championship', my score would have placed me second in an open shoot. I thank Mick for the coaching.

With his mate's property sold, Mick was yearning to go back out onto the land. He commenced his search for a hobby farm, Brenton inspected a couple of places in the New England region of northern New South Wales that Mick found in a 'sell by owner' publication.

As Brenton was now in Queensland, Mick drove up to visit him, together they started to look at possible places. While he was away, I became very ill, my gall bladder had ruptured and I was in danger of sepsis, an urgent visit to ED at the hospital, I was extremely lucky the doctor recognised what was going on and admitted me immediately, I was put on intravenous antibiotics, needing surgery but had to have the infection controlled as a priority. The relationship we had built with our local vet saved the day for our business, a phone call to him had him send one of his veterinary nurses to take care of the cattery while I was sidelined.

Mick completely unaware of what had happened while he was gone, on his return enthusiastically told me he had put in an expression of interest to purchase a place near Kingaroy. When I got the details of the place, I thought he had completely lost his senses, it was just plain ludicrous to think that at our age we could tackle this proposition. The very idea that we could go and live in a cave, in a gravel pit while we built a home, tamed the scrub and established a hobby farm at our age was a complete fantasy. This time even with the caravan I stood firm and said no, this will not be happening. Besides I was still recovering from the recent surgery. Fortunately, there was a cooling off period and we were able to exit the agreement. Still sure that the right place would come up if we were looking together, he eventually persuaded me to sell up in Broken Hill.

The 'For Sale' sign went up in the morning and our neighbour sitting on his front porch said he'd be sorry to see us go. That evening a couple we had known since our dog fence days came to collect their pets, seeing the sign they asked for details, they made a full price verbal offer on the spot and signed a formal contract to buy the house and business next morning. Our neighbour couldn't believe his eyes when the sign was taken down, he thought it must have been by vandals for sure.

Perhaps it was fate or that wind of change decreeing that we needed to move again. We had a month to pack up and vacate, hook up the caravan again and head back into Queensland in search of the 'impossible' dream. The removalists came and loaded up our furniture and effects which went into storage in Queensland. We took our blue heeler dog 'Victor' and our cat 'Rani', a bantam hen and her chick with us, Rani was a chocolate point Burmese. She had been adopted by us when the young man who owned her found that living with a cat and a bird wasn't that good a combination. Especially when his girlfriend was allergic to cats into the bargain. We parked the caravan at Brenton's residence and moved in with him and his fiancée while we searched for our 'utopia'.

Victor got lost while we were staying there, he must have gone after a 'Roo and got disorientated, wandered off in the wrong direction. The area was quite heavily timbered and he was used to open plains. We put up flyers everywhere, and did letterbox drops, have I said that Victor was deaf? Mick always worked him with hand signals, he'd been kicked by a beast when he was very young which may have caused his deafness, or he may have been born that way. This naturally complicated trying to find him. Mick had registered him and our phone number with an animal organisation when we had moved to Broken Hill, this saved the day, we got a phone call; Victor had been found by a family on the other side of Clear Mountain, they had almost driven over him, he was laying on the edge of their driveway in long grass completely exhausted, he could barely stand.

Mick and Brenton went to fetch him, we were so relieved to have him back. He had walked from Cashmere to Dayboro in the valley some 25km away, goodness only knows how many kilometres he had covered in the time he was lost, the poor dog was so footsore he couldn't walk for days afterwards, Mick kept his muscles from stiffening up too much by making him swim in the pool. Victor had never really befriended another dog other than his love matches, Christine's dog Remmy was a gentle soul and gave Victor sloppy licks, they became good mates once Victor recovered. Not so the cats, Brenton's cat Cassie made sure that Rani knew who was boss and kept her in her place.

8

The Western Darling Downs

Deciding we wouldn't go out any further from Brisbane than a day's travel, we drew a circle on the map to outline our search area - we would look at nothing beyond Roma. I made a lot of phone calls to estate agents in country towns, they had nothing that was in our budget, just big farms on the Darling Downs or town lots. Finally, an agent in Chinchilla remembered that he'd had a listing for a small property between Chinchilla and Miles, he rang the people and it was still on the market, so we arranged to go out and inspect the place. What he told us met the criteria that we had set ourselves, it was close to 2 towns, there was good access, it bordered the Warrego Highway on one side, had a sealed access road. There were services, phone, electricity and mail delivery. It was fully fenced with paddocks and dams. There were outbuildings and yards. It had been set up as a working farm, had been a piggery and goat farm. There was a liveable cottage, it was parkland cleared.

We drove out to do an inspection. Mick didn't take much notice of the cottage; he was more interested in everything outside. I inspected the cottage with the lady of the house, she had an air of desperation about her, she said that her hopes of selling had been dashed too many times, she had almost given up hope and contemplated walking away. She told me she was desperate to move for family reasons.

Telling me the history of the cottage she explained that it had been built from timber harvested from the property in three stages while they lived in a converted bus. Firstly, they had built the central section, the long room, it had served them well as extra living space initially, it now served as the living-dining room, then two bedrooms were added. Finally, the bus was taken away - the newest section was built, comprising the bathroom, small storeroom, kitchen and the main bedroom. There was an outbuilding by the house dam where she said her father had lived. Lastly there was an enclosed front verandah with sleepout and an enclosed back verandah housing a laundry and back porch, (where the hot water system stood pride of place - it desperately needed screening. A carport, garden shed, old outside dunny and a pergola over a garden covered by choko and passionfruit vines completed the picture. Outside were two rainwater tanks and an enclosed tank stand with a shower set up under the overhead tank which was filled with dam water.

Mick was convinced that this would be the place, we could create a nice comfortable home here and have the few animals he yearned to have. I wasn't as convinced as he was, in fact I was full of trepidation, but I could see the eagerness in his eyes and agreed, we'd give it a go. I didn't want to be here, having given up my business, the lovely house and garden we'd left, the friends and interests and everything Broken Hill had offered, I just didn't want to be here. I know it was illogical to blame the place I had agreed to come to for the inner sense of loss and anger I was feeling. I hoped my feelings would change over time. We named the little farm "Newgrange"; it was on Brownlies Road, Columboola via Miles.

Columboola is an Aboriginal name meaning plenty of white cockatoos. It is a stop on the railway line heading west and was named after the Columboola Creek. It was a support centre for local farms. The first school had opened in 1896.

The little township came to prominence during WWII, when a munitions storage facility and demolitions range was established adjacent to the railway line with a camp for 50 men, which was utilised during 1942-45 by US forces. In June 1945 the facility was converted to a gas depot. Records show that chemical munitions were stored there between 1943-44. The facility was manned by US service personnel. After the war local residents occasionally found munitions at the site which were removed and destroyed by the Australian Army. By 1976 the population had shrunk to 72 persons, the towns of Chinchilla and Miles having taken over as district centres. The school was now being used as an Environmental Education Centre and meeting place for the occasional family get togethers. It was there that we were invited to meet the local people who welcomed us to the neighbourhood.

The property we purchased was part of the old town site. In the 'recreation' paddock facing the highway was a sporting oval with post and rail fencing, now in a dilapidated state, a buckled concrete cricket pitch in the centre. The outer perimeter of the oval had once been used for picnic race meetings we were told by the locals. There were remnants of a couple of tennis courts to one side, bits of the umpire's stand and bitumen still visible among the grasses. The most outstanding features of this paddock were the two large quandong trees, standing out among the cypress, ironbark and bloodwood trees. The sporting facilities had once been a happy place utilised by locals and the US forces stationed there.

The house block faced a sealed arterial road. A school bus served the area taking children to Miles for primary school and Chinchilla for high school. The old townsite was made up of five and ten-acre blocks. Our back paddock had been gazetted on the town plan as Recreational Common. There was a right-of-way and a lane at the southern boundary which we later purchased to add to our acreage. Total area of our little farm 30.3 hectares or 75 acres. The land was light sandy loam not considered suitable for cropping, colloquially known as a 'prickle farm'.

The name was apt, it grew burr, mainly khaki burr, galvanised burr where the Poplar Box trees grew as well as wire grass under the cypress. The common had been taken over by cypress saplings and had to be cleared again in order to run livestock. The house block was divided into three sections: one for the house, one for the hay shed, general purpose sheds and piggery buildings, and the final third was pasture. Each section had a dam for water storage. The land was flat, gently sloping down towards the Columboola Creek.

The dams and catchment drains were badly silted up and shallow, the piggery was in a poor state of repair, the yards had all but collapsed and the fencing was as poor an excuse for a fence as any I'd seen. The poultry pens not much better. The previous owners had given up, sold their livestock and worked in town for the local Shire. They did leave us a couple of wrecked cars, the chickens, ducks and geese. Also unbeknown to us at the time, two goats which had 'gone feral'. They lived in the adjacent scrub along the creek and occasionally came to drink at our dam. We didn't know they were 'ours' until a neighbour called and introduced himself, then asked if we could 'do something' with them as they were frequently on his property annoying his sheep. Apparently one of 'our geese' had made itself at home at another farm nearby. I wasn't too sure how these were our problems, why had this not been resolved with the previous owners? Surely between them the men could sort it all out. A fox attended to the goose problem but I was drafted into the goat dilemma, they became dog meat.

The plant we purchased along with the property was comprised of a crusher, auger and grain bin, (relics of the piggery) and a Ferguson tractor. A couple of pumps to bring water to the cottage overhead tank and to water the livestock at the piggery. There were no watering points in either of the other paddocks, livestock had to walk into the dams via a series of crooked laneways. Part of the property was grassed with semi-improved pasture and couch grass, then to our chagrin we found out that the whole area of Creekside Columboola, in fact most of the district was infested with 'Mother of Millions', a succulent that was highly toxic to livestock, difficult to control as it spread by the plantlets being washed along drains, lodging in every nook and cranny, drought resistant and a prolific seed producer into the bargain. It wasn't just a prickle farm it was a poisoned challis.

The cottage, dark, dingy and filthy dirty. Lost for words I surveyed it from the doorway of our caravan. How was I going to turn it into a habitable home before our furniture and other belongings arrived from storage? There was only one way, get to work. We went into town to the hardware store, purchased mops, buckets, brooms and brushes, detergent and sugar soap, insect sprays to combat the giant spiders and roaches. We took down the curtains and pulled up the carpets, bare floor-boards were a better option, lit a bonfire and got rid of that lot.

The shade-cloth enclosing the front verandah was next. Suddenly light could enter the dwelling and with it went years of dust and cob-webbing. While Mick was busy taking the old pig pens apart, I removed the lining panels separating the 'new room' from the 'long room,' open plan suited me much better. Then I reconfigured the spaces. The new room became our living room and we set up the long room as our dining room and study. Together we washed windows and walls and scrubbed floors. The bathroom needed a shower, we weren't into baths. Mick bought a pressure pump and connected it, modified the plumbing and we had a shower. The old bath and basin had to stay for the moment.

Mick installed a submersible pump for the septic and cleaned the kitchen grease trap. Each morning the kitchen and bathroom smelled of methane gas, what was going on? Then we discovered that the air vent from the toilet and septic stopped under the carport roof, right outside the kitchen and bathroom windows. Urgent extension to the vent and suddenly the smell dissipated. The kitchen hadn't been fitted out, it was a collection of mismatched free-standing units and in addition to a bench top hotplate unit had a 2-element stove plugged into the corner. It was so covered in grease that even with gloves I couldn't contemplate cleaning it, out the back door it went. The rest of the units got a thorough clean, and were reconfigured. Now we had a breakfast bar with stools and the 'fridge fitted into the kitchen. I didn't want it in the back porch or in the meals area where the previous occupants had had their 'fridge. The bench mounted cooktop worked so that would do, we didn't have an oven, but we had our caravan oven to use until we could get one. A new kitchen would have to wait. The laundry was the worst space to clean; they had been using it to process pigs, it was a slaughterhouse, then I tackled the old stove with scalding water and lots of detergent. I put it and the table we found in the laundry out into the little outbuilding by the house dam. It served as an outdoor cooker quite well.

We ordered aluminium framed windows to be made up with clear glass, the old wooden framed opaque ones didn't let in light or a view. Asked the removalist to bring our belongings out from Brisbane. During a visit to Brenton, I was scouring the 'for sale' advertisements looking for a wall oven and grill, jackpot! There it was, a perfect match for our bench cooktop. It came back to Newgrange with us, set on Besser blocks until we could have it installed properly. The kitchen was complete, still mismatched but clean and functioning. Our furniture duly arrived and we moved into the cottage. The new windows, an air conditioner and slow combustion tile fire were next to be installed. Mick mounted a mantel-piece made from an interesting slab of wood on the wall behind the tile fire. The impossible had been achieved, we had a cottage we could live in. Our dog and cat settled in, the cat found out that there was much more than cattery life, venturing as far as the hay-shed and piggery.

The bantam hen and her chick, (now a fully grown rooster) we had brought with us from Broken Hill were happy in the farmyard. The other poultry having adjusted to the new status quo. I loved watching the geese head out to graze and swim serenely on the dam, noisy as they were. The ducks too were a pleasure to watch waddling about, so graceful on the dam. Chickens scratching and clucking about made for an idyllic scene. The van was parked alongside the utility sheds and the front yard was clear. Then the real work began, we had to get the little farm into shape so that it could function as intended. We made a list of priorities, boundary fencing, internal fencing, gates, yards, watering points, etc. Number one was cleanup.

Mick had a scrap-metal merchant out from Chinchilla and the clean-up was underway, we had filled the trays of the Utes with old rusting fencing wire, netting and empty oil and fuel drums, the wrecks were loaded. The piggery was next, the farrowing crates had to go as well, a reminder of misery, and an assortment of old roofing iron, it was a relief to see it all gone. We ordered gates, straightened and repaired fencing, started to clear the regrowth out in the back paddock, a tree fell the wrong way and a piece of cypress stuck into Mick's hand trapping him, just like when the vehicle falling off the jack needed a swift response from me, I learnt to use a chainsaw to free him. A terrible infection followed, fortunately the spike of wood missed the bones and tendons, so once the treatment to clean the wound and antibiotics had done their job he recovered. Next, we booked the Council plant to cut new drains into the dam and had the house dam cleaned in time for the first rains, finally had a good supply of water. The pumps failed, silt had wrecked the impellers, so new pumps had to be purchased.

Now it was time to look around for employment. I did casual jobs, cooking for a shearing team, part payment a small flock of elderly sheep. House cleaning, ironing, whatever was available. Mick started to caretake farms, check the waters and gates, keeping an eye on the livestock and feeding and exercising the farm dogs. We did a season of cotton chipping, met some interesting people in those teams, we had a colourful fun time with us being part of this motley crew. Assisted with feeding hay and grain to sheep and cattle on neighbouring farms. Helping out at grape pruning, our vigneron tried his hand at wine making, it wasn't good, his sister said that it tasted of straw. He named the vintage 'Hay-shed Broom'. In ensuing years, he sold his grapes to a winery.

The locals became our friends, it was nice to see familiar faces again. I was invited to join the garden club and enjoyed the monthly meetings hosted at affluent farms, with ample water and good soil. Back on our place we continued to make improvements with the help of Brenton and Paul during their visits. The old yards and loading ramp were beyond repair so they were demolished and Mick built new pens and a loading ramp in part of the hay-shed. The piggery became a shearing shed with undercover yards, utilising the repaired old pig pens. We were reunited with old friends from our dog fence days, Godfrey and Virginia, Eoin and Fiona. Unbeknown to us they had settled in the area as well, we were neighbours again, Godfrey and Virginia just a couple of kilometres down our road, Eoin and Fiona managing a property on the other side of Miles. Their daughter Kathleen and her husband had bought a place in a subdivision of 100-acre unimproved lots, youth, enthusiasm and energy enabling the future development of their farm. They started out with a relocatable house. Timber framed houses were transported to new sites, re-stumped, plumbed, then renovated, there were many to choose from in Queensland.

We continued to clear the scrub, undertook weed control of the noxious succulent, planted saltbush and seeded improved pasture varieties, Mick put in fire-breaks, ploughed contours to hold moisture longer, slowing run-off. The seasons weren't good, it was declared a green drought, just enough rain to germinate seeds and put a green tinge over the country, but not enough to fill the dams or follow up for the grasses to mature. It affected the whole district. We had started our livestock venture with a small mob of weaner cattle, aiming to grow them on to store cattle for sale, we turned them off early. A number of the smaller holdings like ours set up feedlots, raised a few head of cattle that way. We kept two heifers, once mature, they were artificially inseminated and we had Murray Grey calves. Our merino sheep were added to by some poddy lambs we were given. The wool was terrible, full of wiregrass seed, so not worth much. The buyer took it just to be kind. We had to supplementary feed the animals with hay and grain, so Mick built a hay rick for the cows. The dams were so low that we started to cart water from the creek. We gave the sheep to a neighbour, a retired shearer. Mick and Paul built me a garden bench using old wagon wheels for the sides, it was lovely to sit out by the firepit some evenings.

There were lighter moments, it wasn't all gloom and doom, in spring the sight of lambs playing and calves suckling was a delight, so too the poultry displaying their young, the broody hens with little fluffy chicks, the ducks with yellow ducklings, and the geese with cute little goslings. The youngest goose had made her nest alongside one of the hens, when the chicks hatched the silly goose took them under her wing, soon the goose with her chickens were in the farmyard walking about with the hen following along, each time they sat the chicks would gather under the goose's down – the poor hen sitting alongside. This continued for a few days, then the hen gave up and rejoined the flock. Further confusion naturally followed when the goose decided it was time to go out onto the dam – now she was confused as the chickens just sat down on the bank, it was amazing that any of these young birds reached maturity.

Then I got what I'll call my lucky break. I applied for a mature age traineeship in horticulture with the Shire and was chosen, given the opportunity to study, had a guaranteed income for 12 months and the possibility of ongoing employment. Finally, I became a professional gardener. It meant leaving Mick on his own during the day but we had our mobile phone and Paul bought him a cordless phone with a long-range base station so he could take the handset out with him. We could still communicate and he had a line out if anything went wrong. Brenton had given him an answering machine when we set up our business in Broken Hill. Our menagerie was destined to grow, another cat. I told Mick it was only 'till I could find her a good home, he responded with 'I think she just found it'. I distinctly remember telling her that she was to live in the hay-shed and outbuildings, but she soon forgot and I found her sleeping in the middle of our bed. Meanwhile I persisted with our garden, it was improving and looking more established. I grew vegetables and installed a micro irrigation system; ants blocked the emitters, silt from the dam water blocked everything else. Using a sprinkler resulted in a grey film covering the leaves so it was back to the old system of flood irrigation.

We had a surprise visit, friends from Gelorup, a real blast from the past. They stayed for a few days before continuing with their travels. Barbara and David came to visit as well. I was so happy to see them, it was wonderful, sad though when we farewelled them getting on the bus back to Brisbane. It felt lonely going back through the gate into Newgrange, the sign above the verandah didn't feel welcoming. Brenton and Christine were occasional visitors, busy with careers in the city. We went down to see them whenever we could. They had married, Paul was best man for his brother. My mother had come over for the wedding and our niece Andrea and her partner Ken came from Adelaide. It was a lovely wedding held in the village of Samford just out of Brisbane. Mother, Andrea and Ken stayed on afterwards and came out to visit us at Newgrange.

When East Timor experienced a humanitarian and security crisis in 1999, Australia led a multinational peacekeeping force in response. The International Force East Timor INTERFET was the largest deployment since the Vietnam War, commanded by Lieutenant General Peter Cosgrove AC, MC. Brenton serving in 1JSU was part of that deployment. Christine newly married was distraught at his going, thankfully he came home safely. The following year Paul married, Brenton and Christine made sure we would be at his wedding, our air tickets to Perth were his wedding present. David lent us his car for the duration of our trip. Andrea and Ken came too. It was wonderful to see my family again, they had all visited us at Newgrange, but it was somehow different seeing them on old familiar ground. The following year Paul's son was born, Che` Michael had joined the family, he was so tiny, Erin brought him to Brisbane so that we could get acquainted with our grandson and he could meet his uncle and aunt.

My traineeship had gone well, I had done extra study and was fully qualified, now held a Diploma in Horticulture, Mick had supported me 100% and had come to Toowoomba with me for TAFE workshops. The mini getaways were nice, Toowoomba a very lovely place to visit. I was offered a full-time position on the parks and gardens team with the Shire, suddenly I was feeling more at ease, surely Newgrange had come through and things would be better from here, not so much of a struggle. Mick could enjoy his farm and I was happy to support him in his dream. I had finally found my true vocation, working in the gardens of the little town, it felt that I was contributing to the community and belonged, it began to feel like home.

The following February 2003, it was a Sunday morning, my world fell apart; Mick suffered a heart attack. I rang 000, it took a lifetime for the ambulance to come from Miles, just 15km away. I saw them drive past our turnoff, still on the phone they were directed back to the intersection, instead of turning left they turned right, away from us, finally they arrived at our front door. Mick was terribly ill, it was bad. They took him to hospital, me following in our car. I went to him in Emergency, was told to wait outside, I flatly refused, a chair was placed behind the bedhead and I was allowed to stay.

Mick was barely conscious, only just aware of what was going on around him, the staff a flurry of activity, the doctor was on the phone to the cardiologist in Toowoomba, they needed Mick's permission to administer a drug. He managed to nod; they still hadn't stabilised him. They ordered the plane to take him to Toowoomba, there were storms brewing, it was going to be a rough flight. I was told to go home, make preparations and head to Toowoomba to be with him. Then someone asked if there was 'anyone' they could call for me. Brenton was away on military exercises; I gave them Christine's number. Acting on auto pilot I rang a neighbour and told them what had happened. They came over and helped me get ready, saying they would take care of everything on the farm and I should just go.

I don't remember much about the drive to Toowoomba or how I found the hospital. Christine was there to meet me, together we waited outside the CCU, (cardiac care unit) not knowing was unbearable. She wanted to call Brenton, I said no! we had to wait until we had something concrete to tell him, same applied to Paul and my family. We waited. A social worker came to see us, allocating us a room in the hostel for families of country patients. Finally, I was allowed to see him, deathly pale and exhausted, hooked up to monitors and with drips in his arms. He was alive and conscious; I turned to jelly as the adrenalin rush passed, I cannot express the feeling of utter relief that overwhelmed me. As ill as he was, his concern was for me, he managed to extract a promise from me, he insisted and I quote "promise me that if I should have a turn for the worse, and not pull through that you will not give up, not stop living, that you will go on", adding he knew I had a lot more to do and experience before my days were done. Words that I'll never forget and a promise I had to make, how could I not after an experience like this. He was in CCU for three days; then they moved him to a ward, it was then that I let the family know what had happened.

Christine stayed with me overnight, but then had to go back to Brisbane, it was a busy time for her at work. I had to keep busy to distract myself and deal with the stress, I cleaned and tidied the hostel, the common rooms and kitchen. I spent a lot of time in the Chapel praying that I could have him longer, he was my kindred spirit, I didn't feel strong enough to face life alone, I felt so small and helpless. As soon as I was allowed, I spent every waking minute at Mick's bedside. I turned 'invisible' the staff pretending they didn't see me anymore; Mick's meal trays came with double helpings. They were very compassionate and caring. Finally, after a million tests, the angiogram result was the worst, the doctor showed me how much damage had been done to Mick's heart muscle. He had lost a lot of its function, too late for stents now. Time would tell how well he recovered. They prepared a management plan and prescribed medications. He wasn't to drive for three months but I could take him home at last.

My employers had been more than supportive, they gave me as much time as it took to get Mick settled into the routine of medication and the management plan became routine. He tired easily but appeared to get stronger. I went back to work; I'd used all my sick leave. I was due for annual leave in April, and had some accrued RDOs so we decided to go to see the family. This time the dog and house cat went into boarding kennels in Toowoomba. Neighbours took care of the rest. We left the car with Brenton and flew to Western Australia. Mainly staying with Paul and his family, also with my sister and her husband, they now had a new house under construction and were in a rental having sold their home. We caught up with some friends, Mick also with ex-colleagues, not wanting any of them to know he'd been ill. There was a shadow hanging over him, he spent a lot of time with our little grandson, took him for a walk each morning, combining his daily exercise regime with enjoying the early mornings by the Australind Estuary.

Then it was time to go back. We collected our pets from the kennels and went back to Newgrange. Mick had to have regular follow-up appointments over the ensuing months. With our Merino sheep relocated, Mick recalled a breed of sheep that had been trialled in the West, Damara sheep, they were a shedding sheep, didn't need shearing and were bred for meat. They had fat-tails, a food store similar to a camel hump. They didn't need improved pasture, browsed more like goats, had a strong herding instinct and were easy to manage. We found a breeder and purchased a foundation flock. A ram and five ewes, they soon had their first drop of lambs. Mick was happy with his cows, calves and Damara sheep.

Concernedly Victor had developed a cough, we were worried that he may have picked up kennel cough in the boarding kennels. Mick took him to the vet; the news wasn't good; Victor had an enlarged heart and fluid on the lungs. His narrow escape from 10-80 poisoning and a subsequent bad experience with paralysis tick had taken a toll. Medication gave him some relief but there wasn't a cure, time was running out. Mick had an appointment to see a specialist in Brisbane, they had discussed a procedure to try to kickstart the damaged portion of his heart, it was still experimental but Mick thought he had nothing to lose so it was worth a try, if it worked, well and good; if not he'd be no worse off. Victor's cough got worse; he was struggling for breath, two nights before Mick was due in Brisbane; Victor died.

We buried him in the morning by the front gate, where he used to lay and wait for me to come home from work each afternoon, then left for Brisbane to Brenton and Christine's home. Mick had paperwork that needed attention prior to his visit to the clinic next morning, Christine witnessed his signature and we had a family dinner. Next morning, she dropped us off at the hospital. Mick did the tests; whatever the procedure was, nothing had changed. I viewed the scans with the doctor who explained the result while Mick was in recovery. Later we enjoyed a limo ride down to the Gold Coast and went out to lunch, Mick had a follow-up appointment that afternoon. The doctor told us that although nothing had changed, with the medication he was on there was no real cause for any concern. Mick said he felt tired but otherwise okay. We returned to the house planning to head home next morning, after having new tyres fitted on our Ute in Toowoomba along the way.

Mick went to sit out on the garden bench, he was very quiet, he must have been very disappointed and feeling the loss of his dog, for 15 years they had shared a lot, an inseparable unit. Christine was preparing dinner; Brenton and I went to the shop for something Mick had asked me to get. When we got back Christine was sitting on the garden wall at the front of the house, Brenton went over to her, I went out the back garden to find Mick, he had collapsed on the paving by the pool, he wasn't with us anymore; I called out for help, someone called the ambulance, Brenton started CPR until the ambulance arrived, they tried the defibrillator; nothing! He was gone, time stood still. We sat with Mick well into the night, a young police officer sitting unobtrusively to one side, (later I wondered why he was there) then the coroners' team came and took him. The three of us left numb, Christine said to me 'I have nothing to give you but the company of my dog tonight'. I understood what she meant, someone warm, living and loving to hold on to.

> It was the night of 8th October 2003, 4 days before his birthday, he should have turned 64.

When daylight finally came, we had some very hard phone calls to make. The family gathered, Mick's mate came down from North Queensland, eventually everyone headed out to the farm, how I got there or who drove our Ute I can't recall. Perhaps it was Mick's mate. Newgrange; now a desolate place with a black cloud hanging over it, made even worse by Victor not being there to greet us.

* * *

Living in a black haze

I remember very little about the next few weeks, yet somehow remember it all, like a slow-motion silent flickering old movie reel. My family had gathered to help me and our sons through this nightmare. Barbara and Christine fed everyone, beds were set up and a cot appeared for baby Che`. Our neighbour across the street opened her home to us ensuring enough accommodation for everyone. All of the neighbours were so kind and helpful, sincere in their wishes of condolence. My employers again supportive, in the extreme.

We had to make arrangements, I floated in a haze between my two sons as they arranged it all. Barbara handled the eulogy with great care, she asked everyone what was important for them to say and how they wanted Mick remembered. A neighbour took care of the printing. On the day we went to choose Mick's coffin, the funeral director told us that as he was bringing Mick back to Miles, he'd had a very strange experience, as if from nowhere a blue heeler dog appeared and trotted down the middle of the driveway. When he turned into the back yard the dog had disappeared. Perhaps Victor's spirit had been waiting for Mick and they were reunited. The man had no reason to tell us this story as we had never met him before. He couldn't have known that Mick had had a blue dog. Time was standing still yet racing by at the same time. We spoke to the priest who would be conducting the service, each in turn, so that he had an understanding of the man he would be burying. Flowers were ordered, pall bearers chosen, his two sons, two old friends and two new friends. Music; we each selected a special piece. The little church was surprisingly full, Mick had touched a lot of lives in the short time we were at Columboola. The graveside service was surreal, Mick was buried with a bit of soil from Newgrange, his 'Town' hat, his dog's collar and his horse's bridle, three things that symbolised what he may need in the afterlife. The wake at the hotel for friends was well attended, the wake at Newgrange lasted all night.

My family who had been my support needed to resume their lives and gradually dispersed; Mick's mate asked me for a keepsake, I told him to choose his own. He picked the plaited belt Mick had made during the flood in Thargomindah; told me he would hold it dear. I thanked him for his support and hoped to see him again soon. The last to leave were Paul, Erin and baby Che`. My neighbour, Wanda who had opened her home to my family moved into the guest room. Her lease was up and she didn't want to leave me alone, her horses came with her and so did her two dogs. It was comforting for a while but then she had to move on as well.

The poor cat, her fur wet with tears, lost as I was, she was Mick's cat and missed him terribly. I had to go back to work and face reality, I was alone and it was up to me now, I needed an income. The cloud didn't lift, I had never felt so alone. I had never been truly single; I had gone from living in the family home to the regimented world of the nursing school then into marriage where we were a partnership. I was facing an entirely new challenge, responsible for myself. I had lost my mantle of confidence, I was the little foreign girl again, unsure and scared of the future, I was second guessing myself constantly and reluctant to make any decisions. I was living yet not, barely managing, functioning on autopilot and muscle memory. Barbara was my rock, she listened to my heartbreak, gave me sound advice on many occasions, never judged and always made time for me. Brenton had his own heartbreak and grief, so did Paul. I knew that from when I'd lost my father, different circumstances but still the same.

'Don't lean too heavily on your children, they have their own loads to carry'. Was something I'd read, that was certainly true now.

Three weeks later I went back to work. Everyone was so kind; I didn't know how to respond. I still felt completely numb yet knew what to do and how to act. It was as if some other force had taken over my body. Then our wedding anniversary brought me undone all over again, for 37 years we had been together, only death could us part, did it really work like that? I didn't think so, I would be married to him until the day I was gone. He had been everything to me, my best friend, husband and lover, father of my children, my world had revolved around him completely, now half of me was missing, an abyss - nothing in its place, just a black haze remained. I should have been a tiny bit thankful; I had been granted eight more months with him, but the final parting hurt so much, I didn't get to say goodbye. Now there was no other option but to carry on, I had made him a promise, there were animals that needed to be looked after, the garden we had planted needed care, some responsibilities don't go away and you have to face them. A routine had to be re-established. Christmas was coming, what would I be doing this year? Friends from the dog fence were emphatic that I should spend Christmas day with them. Their family was going to be together in one place this year, they wanted me there with them. I complied and thanked them for being so thoughtful and kind.

The following Easter I flew to Cairns, our friends from the Territory had settled on a property up on the Atherton Tablelands. Mick had planned to take a trip up to see his mate, he couldn't do it now so I went instead. They were very hospitable and took me sightseeing, I had a very pleasant time with them. The rest of the year passed as before; I was living in my shroud of mist, I decided to finish the renovations to the cottage that we had planned.

Firstly, I moved our bedroom furniture into the guest room, the front bedroom now became the guest room. This room was bigger so I also moved the desk and computer into my bedroom. I purchased a big soft easy chair and set it by the tile fire, this became my safe place, I spent many hours sitting in that chair looking at the dancing flames, remembering and reliving our life together. Then I bought a kit form kitchen and a new stove. Evenings I assembled the cabinets, uppers and lowers, one weekend a work colleague drove me to IKEA south of Brisbane to pick up benchtops. I purchased 'wet-wall' sheeting in a marble tile pattern for the splash-back, not realizing there were two sheets in each box I had inadvertently got enough to clad the bathroom as well.

Brian a neighbour who was a licensed owner-builder installed it all for me. The new stove didn't need to be hardwired; it had a 3pin plug so was an easy install. Then Brian and I tackled the back porch, I moved the laundry out to the outbuilding by the dam, re-purposing the old kitchen cabinets. He gutted the back porch and rebuilt it, I now had a small closet size pump room, and a study which could be used as an extra guestroom. I bought kit furniture and built a cupboard and a nice corner desk; the single bed made a divan when not in use. Moved my computer out of the bedroom. The rear entry porch was big enough to house the freezer. It was a huge improvement, especially after fitting the new back door and window. I filled the old sleepout on the front verandah with seating and plants, a pleasant sun trap on cold winter mornings.

I lost all track of time during the 3 years after Mick left this life. I remember doing things and going places, I recall who came to visit, what was happening in the lives of our sons, but have no idea of the order in which any of it took place. The black haze clouded everything. I was promoted at work, to Parks and Gardens Supervisor.

I saved my RDOs and split my annual leave, this gave me two lots of three weeks per year to have a break. Barbara and David enabled me to fly to Western Australia for important family events. Brenton went back to Timor as a United Nations Peace Keeper; he was posted to Sydney for a time; I went down to visit him. He served in Afghanistan, brought me back an emerald and a lovely scarf, I had the emerald mounted on Mick's wedding band and wear it on my right hand.

Paul came to visit while he was working in Gladstone, it was so lovely to have him there, yet so sad that Mick wasn't there anymore, we sat out by the fire till daylight talking and remembering. Some weeks later I drove to Gladstone and we went to Heron Island for the weekend. Heron Island is a coral cay near the Tropic of Capricorn in the southern Great Barrier Reef, north-east of Gladstone. It's a bird sanctuary, it can be home up to 200,000 species, we went on a glass bottom boat tour and saw turtles, and other marine animals, manta rays, clown fish and colourful corals, stayed in one of the beach houses and spent time walking around the island admiring the tropical vegetation and pristine beaches.

In July 2004, Dylan Michelle Bailey arrived, Paul and Erin had a daughter, a beautiful little girl, so tiny. I was there waiting; I remember how overcome with emotion Paul was when he came to tell us the news. Barbara is her godmother, I visited again for the Name Day

Celebration. Both Che` and Dylan wore the Bailey christening gown which had been handed down through 5 generations.

Life at Newgrange rolled along, the animals still needed supplementary feeding, water was scarce, I had hay delivered and carted water from the creek to keep the garden alive. The Damara sheep did well and the cows plodded in and out from paddock to the dam and back again. I hired some help, a chap that worked on a lot of properties doing all manner of farm related jobs, I'd got to know him through my neighbours, John was a godsend, doing the lamb marking for me, fortunately the sheep didn't need shearing, he helped me finish the fencing and anything else I needed help with. The little farm was looking good even though there was never enough rain.

Brenton and Christine were at Newgrange when the Indian Ocean Tsunami struck in 2004. Brenton came to Newgrange alone and brought me a chocolate labrador the following Easter, he didn't stay overnight. The dog 'Milly' was my salvation, I clung to her, loved her with passion. I went to Melbourne for Melbourne Cup, this one was for Mick, it was on his bucket list. I had always wanted to visit the gardens at Heronswood on the Mornington Peninsula so took the opportunity to do so on that occasion. Mother came to Newgrange again to visit, we went up into the Bunya Mountains and had a lovely weekend. Brenton and Christine moved back to Queensland, stopped coming to Newgrange, busy with life in the city. I would only see them if I went to Brisbane.

I had got to know quite a number of people in town, they recognised me through my work. I joined the book club at the local library, went to art exhibitions and to shows, plays, music revues and concerts, sometimes alone or with my neighbours from adjacent farms. Mick had told me once if you want to know what's going on in any town there are two places to go, one is the local pub, the other is church. I started going to church again, it made me feel at peace, our parish had been without a minister for a few years, the travelling priest only came rarely. On Easter Sunday I met our new resident priest, told her that I had found her sermon very moving. The new Minister was a lady, her husband a retired Army Chaplin, a Vietnam veteran. We quickly became really good friends; I was appointed church warden. This couple did two things to help me shed the shroud of grief I was wearing. They established a support group for the bereaved, and encouraged me in my ambitions to further my horticultural career. Coincidentally we share the same date for our wedding anniversary.

The bereavement group met monthly, we alternated our meeting at each other's homes, would all bring a dish for dinner or a bottle of wine. After our meal we would talk about how it felt to lose loved ones, what coping strategies we had, where and how we hoped to find peace. We were a diverse group and our loved ones had all gone in different ways. There was compassion, love and support within our little group. Our Minister would read a passage from the Bible and we would discuss how we interpreted it, whether or not it was relevant to the times we were living in now, the scripture being such an ancient text. It led to some interesting conversations.

The other thing they did with respect to encouraging my horticultural ambitions was brought about by their wish to revamp the gardens at the little church. The Minister wanted a labyrinth surrounded by a Peace Garden, with seating for contemplation. I did some research on labyrinth designs and drew up a plan to fit the available space. There needed to be some open space as well for gatherings, the congregation would have a fete or market in the church grounds several times a year. All the existing trees had to be retained. I presented my idea and drawings, all met with approval, the Shire constructed the labyrinth, all the materials for hardscape were donated and plants came from myriad gardens. It was all put together with labour at working bees. The Minister and her husband placed a stone from her family farm at the entrance of the labyrinth, I donated a seat in Mick's memory and others did likewise. The Peace Garden was completed. The two Anglican ministers and I sat in the garden and shared a bottle of wine on our wedding anniversaries. I registered my business name, "AMBEE Landscape Consultations and Garden Design".

One day a neighbour, who had been a mate of Mick's, asked how I was coping, he must have caught me at a vulnerable moment, my guard slipped, because I told him how hard it was working full time and trying to keep things going at Newgrange. He nodded and said he understood that couldn't possibly be easy. He reminded me that the farm had been Mick's passion, I shouldn't feel disloyal if I were to follow my own ambitions. Strangely when Paul had come for the weekend from Gladstone, he told me of a dream he'd had, said he'd dreamt that Mick was in the room and told him not to worry about the farm, it would all be okay in the end.

I laid out a labyrinth in the house paddock, walking the path, the circular pattern helped to centre my thoughts, I would lay out my dilemma on the way in and think about solutions on the way out, my dog walking by my side, often nudging my hand; I finally realised my destiny really was in my hands now, then considering my future, I began to look for employment opportunities in Western Australia, contemplated going back to Broken Hill, I'd really liked living there, soon realised it wouldn't be the same without Mick by my side. I looked at real-estate prices in New Zealand, explored options in Tasmania, then thought about moving into town. It was a nice friendly town and there would be a lot worse places to be.

I told Paul and Brenton how I was feeling. Paul suggested that if I was planning a move, what was wrong with Australind; he had his young family and an investment property that I was welcome to live in. His wife Erin gave me contact details for a landscape company who were hiring. Brenton? I think he was disappointed, he didn't really comment, just shrugged. Christine said a lot, she had always wanted to live on a collective and failed to understand my wanting to leave and my ultimate decision to sell up.

I thought about it at length and the more I did, the better the plan seemed. I sent my resume' to a company in Bunbury and was offered a position, I could start in the New Year. This would give me two months to relocate. If the farm didn't sell, I could rent it out, there were always people looking for a place where they could have a rural lifestyle. I consulted the local real estate agent; he came out and inspected the place, suggested a price which I thought was a reasonable return on our investment. He suggested listing on the Internet, saying it's the best way to advertise. I got a call from a couple who were relocating to Miles, school teachers posted to the primary school for the upcoming new year, they asked if it would be ok for their relatives to come and inspect the property on their behalf. In less than a week I had agreed on a sale; the estate agent hadn't had time to put a sign on the gate. Settlement would be completed within the month.

The stock agency arranged the sale of the livestock, my farm helper found buyers for the tractor and other farm equipment. The poultry and the hay-shed cat were staying, the new owners wanting them. I arranged for the few pieces of furniture and other belongings to be picked up by the removalist and sent to storage in Australind. The new owners had asked if I would include most of the furniture in the sale. That was fine with me, it fitted the cottage and likely wouldn't suit me later. My letter of resignation was met with long faces, my employers were truly sorry I was going but understood why. Our friends from the dog fence helped me pack and took what they wanted from what I wasn't needing anymore. Everything else stayed for the new owners.

I drove away from Newgrange with a heavy heart, Milly and Rani beside me, I stayed with Brenton and Christine until the transport came for my Ute. I flew to Western Australia with my dog and cat in time to spend New Years Eve with Barbara, David and mother. Ready to start work at my new job the following week.

I lived with Paul and his family initially, they were in the process of looking for a bigger home. By Easter everyone was settled, I stayed at his address and he moved into the new home just a few streets away.

My introduction to my new employment role had a very short settling in period, it was a very busy time in the construction industry, the company's main focus was on new housing estate public open space development and ongoing maintenance. Some of the Shire Councils were engaging sub-contractors for parks and gardens maintenance and the company had a number of these contracts. Initially I was looking after just one large estate, by the middle of the second year I was promoted to Maintenance Supervisor for the Company's South West Division, and was eventually looking after contracts from Mandurah and as far south as Albany. Responsibilities grew exponentially and a lot of time was spent travelling between sites. Fortunately, I had competent reliable staff and sub-contractors in place on the majority of the sites, at times I felt overwhelmed by the workload. Most weekends were spent doing site inspections locally and administrative tasks. It was a challenging time career wise, being so busy filled my days, kept me from thinking too much about my loss and loneliness, so enabled me to function in my new benumbed state.

Visits from the Minister with her husband, and former Supervisor with his wife from Miles were a pleasure, it was nice to see them and they seemed satisfied that I was going along okay.

I've been back to Miles once, I hired a car and drove out from Brisbane, called to visit my old CEO and his wife at Dalby, the administrative centre of the new Western Downs Shire, formed since the local government amalgamations. I stayed with friends from the bereavement group, visited my dog fence friends and former colleagues. The cemetery was well maintained, the lawns trimmed and green, cypress trees surround the space, the jacksonia and wattle were in flower, it felt peaceful. I stood gazing at Mick's plaque and looked around, remembering. I contemplated all that had taken place while we lived in the area, how short his dream of a farm of his own with a few animals really was, and the journey it had taken to get him there.

He's not really there, he'll live on for as long as my memory lasts, he lives on through his sons and grandchildren. A poem written by Mary Elizabeth Frye, (from Dayton, Ohio) says it so much better; it reminds me of the promise I made that fateful day.

Do Not Stand at My Grave and Weep

>Do not stand at my grave and weep
>I am not there. I do not sleep.
>I am a thousand winds that blow.
>I am the diamond glints on snow.
>I am the sunlight on ripened grain.
>I am the gentle autumn rain.
>When you awaken in the morning's hush
>I am the swift uplifting rush
>Of quiet birds in circled flight.
>I am the soft stars that shine at night.
>Do not stand at my grave and cry;
>I am not there. I did not die.
>
> Mary Elizabeth Frye

The little farm looked the same, yet different, the trees we planted bigger, the cottage seemed smaller, the new owners have made it their own, we had just breathed new life into it. The sign reading Newgrange Damaras was gone. A new shingle by the letterbox. When I left Newgrange to go back to Western Australia it looked so much better than when I had arrived with Mick, I left to escape the grief, the responsibility, the hard work to keep it all together, the broken dreams and the loneliness. This time I left knowing I didn't belong here anymore. I'll be back one day to join him in his earthly resting place. The black haze has slowly turned to grey, sunshine and blue sky breaks through now and then. It hurt just as much to walk away.

"Grief never ends, but it changes. It's a passage, not a place to stay. Grief is not a sign of weakness, nor a lack of faith. It is a debt we need to pay for connection and love."

I don't know who penned these words, I didn't believe them when I first read them, now I know that it's true, time does change everything.

9

Back in Western Australia

I didn't do particularly well at school, life taught me so much more, mixing, working and living among people of different ethnic backgrounds, the blend that is Australia's population from so many walks of life, many strata of society. Some wealthy, others not, everyone just working hard to get by. Life is the greatest teacher.

As you know if you have read this far, my working life started with a holiday job in a department store, in the toy section as a sales assistant. Definitely not my future, it showed me what I didn't want to be doing to earn a living. Business College and all I learnt there was my foundation. The fundamentals of every career path I followed. Nursing was my vocation, or so I thought. I traded it for marriage and motherhood, nurturing may well have been my true vocation. On my journey I have discovered that I have many skills. Practical ones, the kind you need to survive, resourcefulness and resilience. I tried my hand at a sales career in retail, real-estate and insurance. Our business venture was a truly successful one, we sold something intangible, something that our customers didn't know they needed until it was available, it gave them peace of mind and the knowledge that something they loved would be taken care of in their absence. I'm not sure if it was sales or nurturing of a different kind, or perhaps a combination of both.

My most fulfilling career was in horticulture, at last I could work with my passion for gardening, out in the sunshine, cold or rain, it didn't matter. My love of gardening is still as strong to this day as it was when I was a child, delighted by flowers and fruit, woodlands and grasslands, farms and forests, natures garden that covers our earth and makes it possible for humanity to live on our planet. I didn't want it to end, but end it did. My career in horticulture spanned just 15 years in total, but it did much more than provide me with a living wage. It helped to heal my broken heart after I was left to face the future alone, it gave the people I lived among a beautiful environment to enjoy. It provided a habitat for other living creatures, the fauna who are surviving in our man-made landscape, giving back a little of what we had taken.

***

Redundancy

Redundancy, what a horrible word. The state of no longer being needed or useful, superfluous, passe`. Did I see it coming? in a way I did. The economising at the office was obvious, budget cuts and job sharing, vacancies weren't being filled, I had always had a company car allocated, now there was only one vehicle which had to be booked in advance, shared by the entire administration staff. A roster was put in place for office cleaning.

The company didn't have the forward works contracts that it once had, there was so much more competition for contracts and new development had slowed down, urban infill was the new way. The survival of private enterprise is the ability to adapt and reinvent itself. Our branch was suddenly over-staffed. I had climbed to the top of my tree, from Team Leader to Supervisor and Manager of the Parks and Gardens Maintenance division. I'd shown that I was good at sales, bringing in many extra works over and above our contracts, the maintenance division being profitable.

I had recently accepted a side-ways move and become the Occupational Health and Safety Officer, another qualification to add to my resume`, strengthen my position, or so I thought. I had the foundations of my Business College diploma in 'Office Management', I'd kept up with technology and was computer literate, a Diploma in Horticulture, Project Management and OSH. Company policy was said to be 'last on first off', I could easily have stepped into the shoes of our admin staff, and continued in my current role, I knew the processes and systems of the company, I had been there the longest, and built a network with other organisations within the industry. The admin staff of two were offered job-sharing. I was offered redundancy. Told I was past retirement age and the company thought I should begin to enjoy the fruits of my labours! Embrace retirement.

One month later I was asking myself questions like what am I getting up for today? What purpose does life have? My grandchildren are grown, they don't need a 'Nanna'. I started to renovate the house I live in, it was looking a bit tired and needed repairs and maintenance. Areas of the garden had been neglected and needed some love and attention. I had already replaced my faithful Ute with a little hatchback. My Ute never recovered fully from a smack on the nose when a truck lost its load on the highway and it hit the front, it was never the same afterwards.

My lovely Milly was gone and so was Rani, I have a little tabby cat now, she was a stray from the industrial area where the office is located. She needed a home and I needed a friend, she was the best parting gift. I didn't need the carpark sign with my name on it as a memento, or the wooden block with the logo and engraving thanking me for my service. I sat and read, went for walks, joined a group of same 'stage of life' ladies, looking for a purpose, I didn't find one. I talked to my tabby cat, asked her what the meaning of life could be while sitting out in my garden, naturally she didn't say anything, just rolled over and purred.

I was once again living in limbo. I suddenly felt like 'that little foreign girl' all over again, disconnected and aimless, she lives deep within me and rises up whenever I lose myself. I enrolled at TAFE and did a course in Creative Arts, I'd always liked drawing, painting etc. It was good while it lasted, I liked the learning, but had no ambition to fill a studio with amateur works. I attended foreign language classes, they were enjoyable. The people going to them came in pairs, I didn't meet anyone who shared my interest so didn't make any lasting connections.

It's been my experience that joining a group is fine initially, the new person is a source of interest, they get a thorough interrogation so that the original members know enough not to feel threatened, then they turn back into their comfort zone and the new person is left floundering on the edge. If another new person joins then perhaps the newcomers can pair up – if they are quick enough. Is that how it's supposed to work? The book clubs were much blunter, saying they had enough members and didn't need anyone else, thank you very much! I tried a sporting group for mature people, same story – your mentor is friendly and attentive while you're learning the basics, while the other club members don't miss a beat and just go on like you're not there, or they start an interrogation but don't give away anything about themselves. I've almost given up, perhaps one day I'll try again, I really do want to find a niche, a place I can feel welcome and belong.

I don't have lifelong friends, I moved around so much all those I called a friend were left behind, too much distance between us now, our lives taking different paths. When I first arrived from Queensland, I tried to reconnect with couples from our time living at Gelorup, even a colleague from the Vet Clinic days, a cup of coffee shared and promises to keep in touch, then nothing further heard from any of them. Mick and I were a unit, we shared our lives, he was always enough.

Barbara is and has always been the other constant in my life, we may have been separated by distance and walked separate paths, always aware where each other's life's journey was taking us, when we were together there was never any estrangement, our love for each other kept us together. We lost our mother in 2010; she was only a few months away from her 90th birthday. It was another sad time for both of us, Barbara and David had been taking care of her for all the years I was living interstate, her ashes are resting alongside those of her dear friend Josef at Fremantle cemetery.

Barbara lost the love of her life in 2014, bereft and devastated, as inconsolable as I was in 2003, was I enough of a support to her, as she had been to me? I hope so. I've watched her live in the same cloud of grief, unable to push it away, all I could say was 'I'm here', and tell her 'You can't see it now, it doesn't get better, with time it gets different and you will go on'. She didn't believe me then; I think perhaps she is starting to now.

We have travelled extensively together, our first trip away was to Europe, a river cruise from Amsterdam to Budapest. We added Paris onto the front of the tour, her heart broke in Paris all over again, she had planned a holiday with David to re-visit Paris shortly before his health declined. We added Prague, Berlin, where our roots were, the Black Forrest, Salzburg and Vienna on to the end of that tour, each trip the opportunity to visit Paul, who now lives in Dubai. We've visited our near neighbours, Indonesia and New Zealand. Both interesting places and beautiful in their own ways, learning about the culture and history.

Together we've now been to France, Germany, Hungary, the Czech Republic, Slovakia, Italy, Portugal, Spain and to Britain, the USA and Canada, Russia and Scandinavia, to the Arctic Circle and Switzerland. In the Middle East to Oman and parts of the UAE. All places full of nature's beauty, history, interesting people and places. It's been a wonderful diversion. We've also travelled within Australia, to Tasmania, New South Wales, Victoria and Queensland, explored parts of our own state of 10 regions, all different, we haven't seen all of it yet. Australia is so vast, so diverse, to see it all would take a lifetime.

***

Is there still a purpose?

How do I feel about the future? I feel somewhat dispirited and tired, parts of the last year have been especially difficult, it felt like winter came early and chilled my very soul. Has looking back contributed, was it wise to write about the past? When I was young, I vowed to myself to only go forward and not look back. Lately I've had the urge to revisit places that meant something to me, to trip down memory lane. Has the passage of time made me nostalgic?

When you become a parent, it comes with the responsibility of needing to care, to continue to care no matter how old your children are, when that is gone you experience ambiguous loss, which is a different level of grief, grief of a different kind. Not only have you lost the connection, you lose a part of yourself, another redundancy, not being needed anymore. Much like the 'second loss' that follows the death of your partner, suddenly you no longer fit, you are single, old friends sometimes even family members are unsure of how to be around you, so they drift away and you become isolated, even more alone at a time when you are most vulnerable.

This is what I experienced when I returned to Western Australia and attempted to re-connect with former friends and colleagues, Barbara also experienced this after the loss of her husband. I'm not sure why this happens, perhaps we humans are so afraid of death that we shy away from the bereaved because what they have experienced could be contagious, by avoiding them we hope to protect ourselves from the inevitable.

Autumn has always been my favourite time of the year, the time of harvest, of gentle sunshine and still days, muted colours in the landscape, getting ready to face winter. Am I still in the autumn of my life or has winter already arrived and I don't recognise it yet? Time seems to be flying by, six years have passed since I left the workforce, have I adjusted to being a retiree? I've had a good life, known true love, hardship, sorrow and a lot of happiness.

I don't have regrets for the choices I made, perhaps I could have done things differently, I did the best I could, after all it's all been my first time for everything. I've met lots of people, some became my friends, all of them touched my life. I've lived in some of the most remote yet beautiful parts of this land, as well as by the sea, had the opportunity to travel widely on our earth, the blue marble orbiting in space. Had the pleasures of nature's garden unfold before my eyes, the joys of other living creatures coming into my world, I have surely been blessed.

Who knows if there will be any more chapters or even a postscript. Not long after we first met Mick said he thought of life as a cheque-book, with an unknown number of cheques. "Each day of our life is a blank cheque"; he said, "it is up to us how we spend it. We can do so wisely with love and joy in our hearts, or squander the opportunity and waste a day."

Now you know what happened to that little foreign girl. I believe I've balanced my cheque-book and not wasted too many of my days. What do you think?

About the Author

Angelika is now retired after having had a varied and rewarding working life, with her passion for gardening ultimately leading her to a career in horticulture. She lives a in a picturesque coastal township in the south west of Western Australia with her rescue cat Mitzie.

She has a passion for roses, loves gardening and enjoys cooking, likes learning new things that enrich life. Exploring the world with her sister and meeting new people.

She was moved to write this autobiography after friends expressed interest in hearing more about her life in outback Australia, and persuasion from family to leave an account of her and her husband's many and varied experiences.

This book is a reminder that there is adventure around every corner, no matter which path you choose to follow.

www.ingramcontent.com/pod-product-compliance
Lightning Source LLC
Chambersburg PA
CBHW030549080526
44585CB00012B/322